*Godwits Return*

# Godwits Return

Edited by Margaret Clark

First published in 1992 by Bridget Williams Books
Limited, P.O. Box 11-294, Wellington, New Zealand

© The contributors, 1992

ISBN 0 908912 36 6

Cover design by Mission Hall Design Group
Typeset by Geoff Norman
Printed by GP Print

# Contents

# Foreword

An ineradicable attachment to one's birthplace seems to be universal in human experience. Poems and songs through the ages have embroidered the theme 'there is no place like home'. Even philosophers have grappled with it. In a recent interview in the *New York Review of Books*, Isaiah Berlin ruminated at length on what he termed 'non-aggressive nationalism', and traced the beginning of that idea to the eighteenth-century German poet and philosopher, Johann Gottfried Herder. In Berlin's view, 'Herder virtually invented the idea of belonging.' He thought that belonging to a place and a group was as basic a human need as food and drink. To feel at home somewhere was necessary for human happiness: not to feel at home in one's place of residence meant chronic nostalgia, loneliness and pain. Herder's hymn to belonging, unlike later German versions of the theme, was deeply non-aggressive. He valued variety and cultural self-determination, and abhorred alike cultural imperialists and Enlightenment universalists.

Maori and Pakeha New Zealand poets, musicians, painters and writers have also grappled with the notion of belonging – to each other and to our islands. The terms of that belonging have grown more contentious lately as past injustices haunt us and economic stagnation embitters the debate. However, until recently an equally strong strand in our cultural life has been the opposite: the need *not* to belong, the need to get away from suffocating provincialism and cultural isolation, the need to return to or seek one's cultural roots elsewhere. It was even thought that for some like Katherine Mansfield and Frances Hodgkins getting away was a necessary prerequisite for the full flowering of their talent.

1

The writer Robin Hyde, in her novel *The Godwits Fly*, first published in 1938, focused on this urge to flee the familiar in search of both freedom and the exotic. Envy of the power of flight has informed human literature from the earliest times. For New Zealanders living in the earth's farthest islands, migrating birds have always held a particular fascination, and been a powerful metaphor for human aspiration. The Pacific godwit arrives in flocks in New Zealand usually during the second half of September each year. Their favourite localities are Kaipara, Manukau, the Firth of Thames and Farewell Spit. They stay for about six months to avoid the north-eastern Siberian winter, then make the long return journey. Despite spending half their adult lives in New Zealand, Siberia is home to the godwits, for that is where they go to nest. The same instinct to return to nest is evidenced in several of the life-stories in this collection.

Other common themes also emerge from the contributors. New Zealanders are still adventurous and curious – after all, our forebears, whether Maori or Pakeha, had the courage to get up and go. Seeing the world, getting your overseas experience, is still taken for granted as a part of growing up in New Zealand. It is recognised, too, that particularly gifted individuals are likely to need to go overseas for further training and experience. A pool of three million people cannot provide the expertise to nurture all talent, nor sufficient competition and opportunities for display to goad genius to fruition. However, going abroad to further one's career is not now seen as necessarily going into permanent exile. Several of the contributors continue their professional lives in the wider world while maintaining their homes in New Zealand. Air travel has contributed importantly to this possibility, as have modern means of communication which lessen our sense of distance and isolation. The growth of a distinctively New Zealand culture in the written, performing and visual arts has also made New Zealand a more comfortable place for creative people to choose to live.

Questions of identity, whether for individuals or groups, are not static but change and grow with circumstance and self-awareness. As Richard Mulgan reminds us, they must be re-addressed and possibly renegotiated by each generation. His ascendant family dramatically exemplifies this truth. His grandfather wrote the book *Home – A Colonial's Adventure* about the significance of going 'Home' when home was 12,000 miles away. His father wrote *Report on Experience* (first published in 1947) in which he wrestled with what it meant to be a New Zealander. He thought Pakeha New Zealanders were oppressed by their isolation and were 'often wanderers and restless and unhappy men'. Whether they chose to stay or go they had within them, all the time, 'this sad inner conflict and frustration'.

The collective message of this book is, I think, that this is no longer so. These writers have seen, enjoyed and profited from what the world has to offer, but have nevertheless understood why they wish to live in their native land. The choice is not as difficult as it was when Europe was at least six weeks away by ship. In a sense successful modern New Zealanders do not face the difficult choice of earlier talented compatriots: they can, in Malvina Major's phrase, 'have both hemispheres'. They can also, as Robin Morrison says, 'see clearly' what it is that makes life in New Zealand worthwhile. In times of loss of confidence in our political masters and their economic management, we tend to lose sight of these truths. These New Zealanders remind us why godwits return.

*Margaret Clark*

3

# Sunny Amey

## Home and Back Again

I first set out to see the world early in 1951. A year before I had booked the cheapest possible berth with the New Zealand Shipping Company. Somehow I scraped together a one-way fare, £67 10s, and set sail in a sweltering six-berth cabin on the lowest deck of the *Rangitiki*.

We were very crowded in tourist class but we were young (I was twenty-two) and we had great fun on the thirty-two-day journey, stopping only at Panama and Curaçao. Our gang could not remain aloof from the occasional concerts. Russell Kerr was setting off to join Sadler's Wells and later the London Festival Ballet Company. He played the hero to my heroine in a version of *A Fruity Melodrama*. I wore brown chocolate-paper eyelashes stuck on with spit.

I landed at Southampton for the train journey to Waterloo Station with around £20 in my pocket and no return fare. I did, however, have these excellent Kiwi friends who knew the ropes, having left a year ahead of me. It was Festival of Britain year and dozens of bargain tickets were lined up on the mantelpiece for the unforgettable performances that were part of the festival. At night the Skylon dominated the South Bank and we were wide-eyed at all there was to see. We danced around London singing 'Mocking Bird Hill', the hit tune of the day!

I had no problem finding work as a supply teacher as there was a shortage in this profession. New Zealand teachers were well trained and we were welcomed professionally and personally with open arms. 'Your boys were wonderful during the war' – we were hailed as heroines because of it. There was still rationing in Britain. We were allowed to take in up to fifty pounds of tinned food. Our gift tins of ham, tongue, peaches and reduced cream brought tears to the eyes of deprived British housewives.

Well, the supply teaching was often a frightful experience, but that's another story. It took me three and a half years to raise the fare back, and then it was only possible with a loan from friends, who had persuaded me to apply for a position at the Wellington Teachers' College, now known as Wellington College of Education Te Whanau o Ako Pai ki Te Upoko o Te Ika. The college was then in Kowhai Road, Kelburn, as it had been in my student days, but that building has long since disappeared and the institution has moved to Karori. Students no longer have the excitement and camaraderie of piling onto the cable car.

I had been a student at the college in the forties and the liberal education I had received there as a student teacher had contributed greatly to my desire to widen my horizons with overseas experience. In the years 1946 and 1947 there were more men than women trainees, owing to the large influx of 'rehabs' – men returning from service in the Second World War. They certainly widened our horizons. They said the freshness and innocence of us seventeen-year-olds gave a balance to their lives after the horrors of the war they had experienced overseas. As a school girl I had corresponded with a brother and a sister in the armed forces, and learnt about Guadalcanal, Cairo (Shepheard's Hotel), Italy (Cassino, Trieste) – all alluring and one day to be explored. After the war I had a German penfriend, Helga. Youth would put the world to rights.

A whole new world of arts and literature (mainly European culture) had opened up to me as a student at teachers' college. Among the tutors were Walter J. Scott, Anton Vogt, Roland Hipkins, Louise Henderson ('Madame' as we called her), and Arthur Barker – all practising writers and artists. They built on that urge to inquire, to search for truth, already developed by the many fine teachers who influenced me at Seatoun Primary

School and Wellington East Girls' College. So other lands were constantly beckoning, but seemed like pipe dreams.

I completed a third year training in speech therapy at Christchurch Teachers' College and then spent two years as a sole-charge speech therapist in Palmerston North. After that I took the risk and began to realise some pipe dreams with that first visit to Europe. I was part of the post-war exodus of young people who had to go to Britain, the country that was still referred to as home.

So in 1955 after that first OE I returned to the college that had led me to so much personal growth and further developed my independent spirit. I was a junior lecturer in English with special responsibilities in speech and drama. One of my principal tasks was to look after the drama club of some eighty or so students who met every Thursday on culture club mornings. I also had to direct the major production, an awesome task considering the then fine reputation of that college's contribution to the cultural life of Wellington.

I had no idea how to direct a play, though I had acted in many amateur productions. First up I chose to do *The Male Animal*, a serious comedy by James Thurber and Eliot Nugent – a play with a political message, written at the time of the McCarthy witch hunts in the United States. Fortunately I could not find one of those French's Acting Editions that showed a picture and ground plan of the original settings and dictated every move and piece of business, mostly quite unsuitable for our small stages. There was only the bare text, so we problem-solved, created the appropriate settings, moved as we thought would be logical, and improvised quite often. Movement and improvisation were a major part of our drama club activities, as I had acquired some skills from courses I had attended in England. I had also been introduced to concepts of theatre-in-the-round, working with child drama pioneers Peter Slade, Brian Way and many others.

*The Male Animal* was a great success. The next year I tackled Pirandello's *Six Characters in Search of an Author* with Grant Tilly, Dinah Priestley and Ralph McAllister in the cast. So many talented students, creative artists, passed through that drama club, among them Jenny Priestley, Laughton Pattrick and Ian Mune.

After *Six Characters* I knew that I really wanted to learn about directing plays. I had always wanted to steep myself in one of the art forms, and theatre was to be it.

I was a member of Unity Theatre and when given the opportunity in 1958 I directed the first ever amateur production of Arthur Miller's *A View from the Bridge*. This play had created a sensation in London, even though performed at a club theatre, when one man kissed another (albeit unconsenting) on stage.

I had applied for one of the overseas grants given by the Department of Internal Affairs (this was pre-Arts Council days). The success of *A View from the Bridge* must have contributed to my gaining one of the coveted awards, then worth £400 a year. Having been given eighteen months to study play direction and drama in education, I took leave of absence from the college, setting off again by sea. Once more the only ship available was the two-class *Rangitiki*. This time I managed to afford a four-berth cabin, one deck up.

At that time theatre schools in Britain did not offer training for theatre directors. In this country the only continuing professional theatre was the New Zealand Players, established by Edith and Richard Campion in 1953. (The company expired in 1960 during a production of *A View from the Bridge* – the necessity to tour had proved too big a financial burden.) In *Plays and Players* and in *Theatre World* I had read so much about the new avant-garde theatre epitomised by the work of the English Stage Company at the Royal Court Theatre in Sloane Square. Established in 1956 by George Devine, this company gave opportunities to new writers. Their first play was *The Mulberry Bush* by novelist Angus Wilson. The second, John Osborne's *Look Back in Anger*, was to change the face of British theatre, mainly through its anti-hero, the angry Jimmy Porter.

A personal letter of introduction to George Devine from his former student Richard Campion gained me an audience with this visionary man of the theatre. I later found out he was besieged with requests from overseas, so I was lucky to be seen. Puffing away on his pipe, the silver-haired George advised me that observing was not the way to learn about theatre. They were short of an assistant stage manager for a Sunday night production.

Would I step in straight away? The director was Lindsay Anderson, the film maker. Thus began my career in the professional theatre, and an opportunity to learn all aspects with a dynamic, progressive group in a delightful small Victorian theatre.

If I earned any money I was not permitted to receive the £8-a-week New Zealand Government grant. So when I was offered contract work as an assistant stage manager at £9 a week I got permission to put the grant into recess – I managed to spin out that bursary over two and a half years. Still, I could not have survived financially in London but for good friends from my previous visit. A number of bursars fell apart with the stress.

I worked for eighteen months at the Royal Court as assistant stage manager, assistant director, research worker and property maker in the workshops. To my surprise the stern-looking John Dexter asked to have me as his assistant when he directed the Wesker trilogy – over five months of rehearsals and performance. Arnold Wesker was often at rehearsals, as were most playwrights at the Court, often rewriting a new play as we went along. *Roots* was the play that really furthered Joan Plowright's career. Soon after that came Ionesco's *Rhinoceros* directed by Orson Welles. By this stage Joan and Laurence Olivier's romance had flourished and they were both in that company. All publicity was forbidden and we had to be very vigilant as the press were hounding them and trying to invade rehearsals. A penniless writer called Edward Bond was given the job of guarding the stairs to the Dress Circle, while reading scripts at ten bob a time. One day he stopped a rather ordinary-looking fellow in the foyer. 'Excuse me, you can't go up there.' I watched in horror, signalling madly from behind. 'It's all right, I'm one of the company,' said Sir Laurence demurely. Poor Edward! He went on to much greater things.

It was extremely difficult for women to work as directors at this time. Apart from Joan Littlewood, there were few others. I was not going to get even a Sunday night production without decor out of George. With an introduction from Bill Gaskill, one of the Court's associate directors, and using my bursary (free apprenticeship), I got work as assistant to the director at the Marlowe Theatre, Canterbury. This was a weekly repertory theatre. Actors began rehearsing Tuesday morning and opened the following Monday, often playing a different play at night. My first production was Wesker's *Roots*. They figured I must know something after working so closely on the trilogy for five months. I was given ten days for this tricky project – the main character Beatie is scarcely off-stage. A number of understudies from the Court came to the Marlowe to have the opportunity to play their parts, although in a rather different production.

*Roots* went so well that Hazel Vincent Wallace, the doyenne director of the repertory theatre at Leatherhead, suddenly decided she might find a place for me after all. Would I like also to direct *Roots* at her theatre in a fortnight's time? I bravely declined. The pace of weekly repertory at the Marlowe was sufficiently gruelling by itself. Some seven months and six or so productions later, I left totally exhausted, but I had learnt heaps – how to see essentials quickly, for one thing.

By this time my leave of absence was up. I resigned from the teachers' college, for I could see there was a great deal still to learn that might eventually contribute to the growth of a professional theatre in New Zealand. I managed to get a few other repertory productions, usually when the management was desperate and prepared to take a risk on a woman. I had to give away my high ideals about only directing plays with a social message. The bread-and-butter learning lay in thrillers, and plays like *Badgers Green*. Who would have thought I'd direct a play about a village cricket match? The dear old actor playing the lead could not learn his lines in a week, a situation I encountered on several occasions, and understood myself when at the Marlowe I had to play the part of Miss Frost in J.P. Donleavy's *The Ginger Man*. I never felt secure with the text – a dreadful feeling. The only other role I played there was in a production of *Pygmalion*, when I had a few lines as the man from Hoxton, converted to a female.

In between times I took odd jobs, including making props for the theatre and some teaching. I actually established the first English-as-a-second-language class for the Inner London Education Authority at a secondary school in North London. This was 1961 and I had fifteen twelve- to sixteen-year-olds from five different nationalities who spoke no English at all. First I drew a lavatory on the board and we all then took a walk to the appropriate place. Then we walked on down to Camden Town and bought some food. Drama and enactment were to the fore. I was flying blind but seemed to stumble on the direct method. They made rapid progress, and it was just getting to the difficult stage when a big theatre opportunity arrived. I was very torn, and wept on leaving my charges.

I had been approached by Pieter Rogers who had been general manager at the Royal Court. Sir Laurence Olivier had agreed to form the first company for the Chichester Festival Theatre, and was to direct all three productions and act in two, rehearsing over ten weeks. Would I be interested to work as the production assistant?

Chichester, a small charming cathedral town near the Sussex coast, was to see the birth of a prestigious summer theatre festival. This concept of local ex-mayor, Leslie Evershed-Martin, was inspired by the BBC film about the establishment of the Stratford (Ontario) Festival Theatre in Canada. Somehow his dream became a reality, but there were nightmares on the way to opening. The new thrust-stage theatre was not finished when we moved the company down from London for final rehearsals. There were constant interruptions and the bulldozers roared relentlessly. Sir Laurence used his considerable charm to negotiate relief for our shattered nerves and eardrums. We were incommunicado for two days after a cable was accidentally cut by the diggers. On the morning of the opening night, 3 July 1962, we found wet tar had been tramped through on the new spring-green carpets. Chichester was scoured for bottles of oil of eucalyptus as we scrubbed away at that carpet.

The first two plays, an obscure Jacobean *The Chances* and the even less performed *The Broken Heart*, were not treated kindly by the critics – they were very against the form of the theatre. In the *Observer* Kenneth Tynan published 'An Open Letter to An Open Stager', damning the new three-sided stage and being rather rude about the programme. (When the National Theatre was formed in 1963 Ken Tynan was invited to be literary manager on the principle, if you can't beat 'em, get 'em to join you!)

At Chichester I was 'Little Miss Fix-it', the liaison and go-between for the various departments, a kind of co-ordinator and soother of ruffled feelings. At times there were lots of tensions and temperaments as we raced against the clock. The saviour of the season was the historic production of Chekhov's *Uncle Vanya* with its illustrious cast that included Sir Laurence as Astrov, Michael Redgrave as Uncle Vanya, and Sybil Thorndike, Lewis Casson, Joan Plowright, Joan Greenwood and Fay Compton.

I shared a house for this and the following season with Rosemary Harris. There were so many receptions and parties honouring the company and the occasion. We called it 'The Champagne Summer', and soon had rows of souvenir corks lined up on the mantelpiece like little mushrooms. In that first season Rosemary asked to understudy Joan Greenwood, as Ilyena, for something to do (she was playing in only one of the three plays in the repertoire). Joan said in her distinctive husky voice, 'I know you're all hoping I'll slip on a banana skin so that the lovely Rosemary can play the part!' There were no banana skins that season, but in 1963 Rosie played Ilyena in Chichester and then at the National Theatre at the Old Vic when it opened in October.

The nucleus of the National Theatre Company was formed from the second Chichester Festival group, with two plays transferring, Shaw's *St Joan* with Joan Plowright as Joan, and *Uncle Vanya*. The long-awaited National opened with Olivier's production of *Hamlet* with Peter O'Toole in the title role and Rosemary as Ophelia. Everyone was cajoled into walking on in the big Court Players scene. I was embarrassed to find that my surname meant I headed the list of servants and courtiers, some of whom were already distinguished actors. I came from below stairs with Colin Blakeley, disguised as a cook, as my partner. We stood in the pit with our backs to the audience. Colin hand-held a spotlight that lit the scene from below and I was supposed to cover the lamp with a cloth every time O'Toole passed in front of it. 'Ya,' breathed Colin nightly, 'you'll have to go. Yer missed again!' One day in the canteen Michael Redgrave (Claudius) said with a sly smile, 'I always enjoy you and Colin in the court scene!'

11

But how can I describe the five and a half years I spent at the National? We always worked at a frenetic pace. Once during a production week I put in ninety hours, sometimes leaving the Old Vic at 2 a.m. and returning at 7 a.m. that same morning. In the beginning I was one of three assistant directors whose responsibilities varied according to the particular director of a production. Sometimes we had quite an input, would be asked an opinion, and could make suggestions. Other times I'd be collecting a director's laundry or fetching his lost dog from the Battersea Dogs' Home – a heart-rending experience that he couldn't front up to, and neither would I again. The dogs all rush frantically to the wires, barking and begging to be rescued.

We rehearsed the understudies and sometimes put in replacements. I rehearsed Mike, a raw-boned junior actor, now known as Michael Gambon. Anthony Hopkins came in from playing leading parts in repertory to be a dancing sailor in Congreve's *Love for Love* and to understudy various roles. As a thirty-year-old he went on with a few hours' notice to play for Sir Laurence as the old retired captain in *Dance of Death*. He never looked back.

In 1965 I was promoted to something called repertory manager (I never signed my contract as I thought it sounded bossy), and I was to work also as assistant to Sir Laurence, who needed someone to remind him about things. This meant I was present at all planning meetings and had to schedule the plays in repertoire. In the mad early days we sometimes had five different plays in a week, as well as others on tour. At one stage Maggie Smith had to be flown by helicopter from Chichester after a matinée to play another part in the Old Vic that night.

In my capacity as Olivier's assistant I was present at many interesting meetings, both professional and social. I once sat in on an hilarious session of reminiscences between three great knights of the theatre – John Gielgud, Tyrone Guthrie and Laurence Olivier. I regret that I did not keep a diary. The offices for the National Theatre were in a long row of Nissen huts on an old bomb site in Aquinas Street, some five minutes walk from the Old Vic. There was a long corridor with rabbit-hutch offices. Sir Laurence had a double where most meetings took place. I had

12

a tiny single opposite, where I was on call as a sounding board, or busy sorting out problems or discussing needs and wants with actors, technical staff and management. My capacity for work was certainly tested – it was a hard slog from 9 a.m. till midnight.

The energy, inspiration and stamina of Olivier never seemed to flag. I had differences of opinion with him when he pushed himself relentlessly beyond even his capabilities. I think my main value to him was that I always said what I thought. My practical commonsense New Zealand qualities were useful. I was respectful but not overawed or sycophantic.

Still, they were special years with many unforgettable memories. *The Royal Hunt of the Sun* had a magnificent *coup de théâtre*, with the awesome opening of the sun revealing the Atahuallpa of Robert Stephens, looking ten feet tall. Sir Laurence's rendering of the 'like to the Pontic sea' speech in the title role of *Othello* still rings in my ears. I would often sneak into the back of the Old Vic to catch these special moments. Noel Coward directed his own *Hay Fever* and said of his cast that they could have played the Albanian telephone directory backwards. During rehearsals we used to rush to the canteen to hear the latest of his witticisms.

In 1965, led by Sir Laurence, a sixty-five-strong company took its first visit abroad. We spent three weeks in Moscow, the first foreign company to play inside the Kremlin. Houses were packed for *Othello*, *Hobson's Choice* (a good socialist play) and Congreve's *Love for Love*. The Russian response was remarkable and very informed. On the way home we played for four nights in West Berlin. I was deeply affected by the contrast between the austerity and restrictions of Moscow and the frantic opulence of Berlin, still divided by the Wall. As in all theatre there were wonderful highs and devastating lows.

There came a time when I just had to get out of England. No matter how fulfilling the life is, as an expatriate there are always days when you pine for your own country – the smell of the bush, the beach, the vigorous mountains, the Pacific light, warm summers. When feeling low I used to say, 'There's nothing wrong with me that the sound of cicadas wouldn't cure!' So I got leave for ten weeks and took my first international plane flight back home in time for Christmas 1967. At that time many New Zealanders seemed to be in awe of overseas achievement. We still suffered from the cultural cringe – anything from the old country must be better. I was disconcerted that people seemed to expect me to be 'grand' because I was Sir Laurence's assistant and had worked with the 'greats' of theatre. I worked very hard to show that I hadn't changed, drinking innumerable cups of tea with absolutely everyone, but my heart and head were still in England. I was a Londoner. I could never return to live in New Zealand, I thought.

One night during this visit friends took me to a small innovative restaurant theatre in Courtenay Place. The meal was indifferent – over-cooked sausages smothered in tomato sauce with cold mashed potatoes. The two one-act plays were competently acted but very dull. My friends apologised, saying it was usually better than this. I loved it. The atmosphere of Downstage was unique. It had been founded in 1964 by Peter Bland, Tim Eliott and Martyn Sanderson with businessman Harry Seresin. Apart from La Mama in New York, there was no other theatre like it in the world. Certainly none in Britain offered dining, with serious theatre to follow. It really gave me a buzz.

I returned to Britain via Sydney and Japan, where I was asked to negotiate for a possible visit of the National Theatre to Expo in Japan, and afterwards to Australia. When I got back to the National the management seemed quite uninterested in my negotiations. The Japanese wanted only Sir Laurence, not seeming to have heard of Albert Finney, Maggie Smith and others in our splendid company. Sir Laurence was not going off to Japan, he said, despite pleas that the country was becoming a significant world power and that it was in our political interests to go. I was rather disillusioned at the cavalier attitude to my findings, but was soon plunged back into the heavy work routine.

Maybe it was the three months away. Perhaps I felt trapped behind a desk, not fulfilling my personal needs, but after five and a half years I no longer felt I was contributing productively to the organisation. Finally, I would wake in a cold sweat in the middle of the night. 'We can't do that because, because . . .' All was not lost, but my quick little computer brain was slipping. I was a burnt-out case. I felt I had come to the end of the road so far as the National Theatre was concerned. It was time to move on.

There was no way I could tell Sir Laurence this face to face. I knew I would get emotional, choke up, be rendered speechless, fail to make him understand, or succumb to his charm. I was a very useful person to him, and I did not stand in awe when there was a bigger cause than his needs. I wrote him a letter explaining that my mind and spirit were atrophying and that I needed a life outside of our theatre. My love affair with the National had come to an end. Separation was essential if a good relationship was to survive. The next day he popped his head round my office door and gently said, 'Well, Sun, how long have we got?'

Some months later I was on a training course for television directors at the BBC. Six years earlier, when BBC 2 was about to be established, there had been a large advertisement in the *Times* inviting applications for trainee directors, production assistants and other personnel. I had applied, gone through a series of gruelling tests and heard nothing for months. By the time I was notified that I had gained a place, I had accepted the job with the National Theatre. 'Never mind,' said the BBC, 'let us know when you are free.' So to ease out of the National I wrote to ask if it was still possible. To my astonishment they said, 'Yes, do come.' I was the only one of the eight trainees from outside the television service and it wasn't easy. On my first morning at Shepherds Bush, where I always felt like an ant crawling into a giant factory, I entered the chief executive's office. I approached a large desk across yards of soft carpet. An elegant man in a pin-striped suit beckoned me into an armchair and then said, 'Well, Miss Amey, you have been a long time coming to us!' British understatement has always been a delight to me.

As part of the training course we trailed on various programmes. I slowly worked out that 'MCU' on scripts meant 'medium close up', but when I asked what 'WHO' stood for there were wide grins as they said, 'Well dear, you *are* trailing on *Dr Who*!' (Patrick Troughton at that stage). I completed the course and did one Thirty Minute Theatre – a comedy, hard to get up on the box. I was not particularly pleased with it. I did not enjoy my time at the BBC. 'You must drink in the club,' they said. 'That's where you meet producers and get the work.' I hated that creepy crawling notion. So I didn't like the BBC before the Thirty Minute Theatre, and I liked it even less without the sweet smell of success in my nostrils.

Towards the end of my six months at the BBC I received a letter followed by a phone call from New Zealand. The chairman of the Downstage Theatre Board, Professor John Roberts, egged on by Grant Tilly, was asking me if I would consider returning to New Zealand on a two-year contract to help build Downstage into a fully professional theatre. I was flabbergasted and intrigued. They were asking a New Zealander, rather than the usual importing of some repertory director from England. They were asking a woman, and they were asking *me*. At long last I could offer something back for the grant that had sent me overseas with no strings attached but in the hope that I might one day return.

I thought Downstage was a gutsy institution, but I had lots of questions and asked for a few days to think about it. The balance was swung by the regard I had for Grant and my real trust that he would be there to work with me. And he was, along with many other dedicated people.

Being sure I was to remain a Londoner, I left my little house with tenants, and after twelve years away I arrived back in New Zealand in September 1970. Wearing a dashing red PVC mac down to my ankles I entered Downstage at the old Wellington Boating Shed with designer and board member, Raymond Boyce. It was a wet southerly day, and apart from my mac the place looked really dark and dreary. I had a rip-roaring post-flight throat and a fever. 'Good heavens,' I croaked, 'how *do* you get away with it?' Raymond was disconcerted. Knowledge of the stringent British theatre safety regulations made me see it as a fire trap with many kinds of physical risks. I think I must have been a real shock with my determination to set professional standards in every aspect, both on and off stage. I was used to hard and dedicated work in an industry that depends on absolute commitment to one another.

Oh, but some really exciting theatre took place in that old boating shed (now smartened up and moved several metres back as part of the waterfront development). When I first arrived, actor/director Nonnita Rees sat looking after the box office. She also edited the exceptional *ACT* magazine. Harry Seresin ran the restaurant operation, and Pat Hawthorne held the administration together. Rats, said to be harmless water rats, danced in the rafters.

My first production was *The Daughter-in-Law* from a trilogy of D.H. Lawrence plays revived a few years previously at the Royal Court. It had only a two-and-half-week season and was completely booked out as everyone wanted to see what the new director could do. I had a splendid cast: Grant Tilly at his naturalistic best, newcomer Janice Finn, Jeanette Lewis as the mother who would not let her son free from her apron strings, and the stalwart Eric Wood, also the theatre's set builder.

At the end of my first year I was asked if I would extend my contract a further two years, making four in all, to see the company through the move into the new Hannah Playhouse. Thanks to the initial generosity of Mrs Sheilah Winn, the new theatre was to rise on the old coffee-bar site of the original Downstage in Courtenay Place. Suddenly I realised I was starting to say, 'We could do this' rather than, 'You could do this.' I looked at my land and its many advantages. The cicadas were singing and the future seemed bright. There was a great upsurge in the arts and crafts, a huge development in pottery and weaving, and a vibrant if struggling theatre. The all-too-brief Norman Kirk years, with some visions for New Zealand, were beginning. My country was wide open with enormous potential to be a positive force in the world. The Maori renaissance had not yet begun but the voices of radical groups like Nga Tamatoa and Te Matakite o Aotearoa were beginning to be heard. During my years overseas there had been a large influx of peoples from the Pacific Islands. The streets seemed more lively with new voices on the wind.

I decided that I did not want to grow old in London, nor would I stay for ever in the demanding, stressful role of running a theatre, perpetually zooped up on adrenalin and having little life outside of it. I committed myself to four years only, and then someone else must have the opportunity to experience running the theatre.

I went back to Britain early in 1972, sold up my house and arranged for my cat, Walnut, to be shipped to New Zealand. On my return I found one of my favourite productions, *Wind in the Branches of the Sassafras*, had grown enormously in the capable hands of a brilliant cast. Downstage at the boating shed was in good heart but was racing towards the big move to the Hannah Playhouse which opened in October 1973 with my production of Shakespeare's *As You Like It*, splendidly designed by Raymond Boyce. The following year six of the main-bill plays were New Zealand works, and they brought in good-sized audiences. This is something of which I am really proud. Thus Downstage fully occupied my life until the end of 1974, when I resigned as I had said I would.

After I left that theatre it took me a full year to recover, to unwind. I went back to Europe for three months. Returning to New Zealand I looked after three adolescent boys while friends went abroad. Finally I was persuaded to apply for a position as curriculum officer for drama with the then Department of Education. It was the one and only full-time appointment for drama ever made by the department. The job was a national one, with responsibility for the development of drama throughout the whole school system. A key component was the building up of resource teachers and drama networks. I was able to combine my knowledge of theatre with my background in teaching. It was a time of growth in education with some emphasis on personal development and concepts of self-worth. Academic excellence is not the only criterion for good citizenship.

It was also a time of growth for me when I became more aware of my identity as a New Zealander. In 1975 I was only the second woman to join the Curriculum Unit, the third being Tilly Reedy as curriculum officer for Maori Studies. I had tutored Tilly at teachers' college – we were connected. I began to look further at cultural issues. Though still attached to head office in Wellington, I moved to Auckland, the city with the biggest population of Polynesian people in the world. I was housed at the Teachers' Centre where I frequently came into contact with Maori and

Pacific Island educators and community workers. I also had the opportunity to do six weeks intensive study in Te Reo Maori at the Kuratini attached to Wellington Polytechnic. All sorts of seeds were sown and many connections were made. I began to see that the saving grace of this Aotearoa could be two peoples standing side by side, sharing the best of the two major cultures in order for all peoples to have pride and self-esteem in being New Zealanders.

No, I am not a bleeding heart liberal! In my opinion this is a term of disparagement used by those who are perhaps too closed or bigoted or maybe too frightened to recognise cultural difference and the qualities and wisdoms that each brings to our community.

During my time as education officer for drama I was privileged to work with quality primary, secondary and tertiary teachers from throughout the country. The drama networks were established and NZADIE, a professional association for drama in education, came into being. After thirteen years back in education I was compelled to retire from the public service on the day of my sixtieth birthday. Sadly, at a time of retraction, the job lapsed. As a consequence some tasks were left uncompleted that might have been polished off by a contract worker. I still regret that, and the lack of recognition of the value of drama in many of our schools. Both children and adults learn through enactment. It is a vital way of coping with and foreshadowing events.

I was just settling down to stick forty years of loose photographs into the albums when I was called to higher service. Would I stand in for a while at Te Kura Toi Whakaari o Aotearoa: the New Zealand Drama School? They needed an interim director with some knowledge of professional theatre and of education. I was also to look at the curriculum and its relevance to a changing society. Graduates of the school have an undoubted influence on future directions for theatre in Aotearoa. I said I could give it a year. In the event I was there for nearly two years, and now I'm getting on with my retirement.

Why did I stay in this country? Workwise it's been a combination of these two professional strands of theatre and education that synthesised most for me in the task I was asked to do at the Drama School.

I seldom talk about the glamorous National Theatre days. I worked in British theatre for ten or so years. I worked so hard I reckon a few nuts and bolts went missing and they've never been replaced! It was a remarkable experience but it's in the past. I was nourished by it but I no longer need to feed on it. I get great pleasure from seeing on film or television young actors I worked with who are now in their maturity, some in their greatness. It's been an interesting exercise to take those years out of tissue paper and find that they have not really faded.

I am content in Aotearoa, yet I still have days when I long for the woods of England and the changing seasons. For some years I was torn between the two hemispheres, but a recent trip to Europe has cured me of that kind of cultural schizophrenia. I know now absolutely that I belong in New Zealand. I love the land, te whenua. I too am bound to it by an umbilical cord. As a child at Seatoun school a teacher instilled in me a love of the children of Tangaroa, the creatures of the sea, and a caring for the bush and the haunts of Tane. On a visit to the great Waipoua kauri forest I reeled back almost fainting in the awesome presence of the great Tane Mahuta. That tree has a huge life force, and so has his mother, Papatuanuku.

The heritage of two major cultures, Maori and Pakeha, and the many ethnic mixes that comprise our people make us unique, but we must all have a place to stand. We have a chance over the next few years of discovering our identity as a country of the South Pacific. This is where our future lies. Despite the tensions and the stresses with the present dismantling of the welfare state, and a retrogression in education, I believe we do have the potential to be a model society. The challenge is to look after the social and spiritual welfare of all our people. We are living in a difficult yet exciting time. Whatever the struggle for a good and just society, I want to be here and I want to be part of it.

# Sharon Crosbie

## A Sense of Wholeheartedness

My early childhood was spent in Rangiora. My grandparents had a marvellous garden and that was my first world to explore. Because I was an only child I enjoyed a good deal of adult company and intellectual stimulation. I also read a great deal. When I think about it, all those books were from overseas and all those stories were about different places. My edition of *A Child's Garden of Verses* was from the United States of America and had pictures of exquisitely dressed children doing exciting and interesting things in beautiful but alien landscapes. Also the woods in which Eeyore and Piglet of the A.A. Milne books had adventures were quite unlike my grandparents' garden. And in *Hans Brinker or the Silver Skates* rivers froze over in ways outside my experience and people wore very odd clothes. One of my favourite books was a Sunday School prize – I still have it somewhere – it was called *How Do You Get There?* It was not about attaining heavenly bliss but about going places. The final picture was of a tiny Chaplinesque figure walking away, seemingly onward for ever.

So very early the seed was planted that it was exciting to go places, to see exotic people living different lives. When you think about it, almost all my generation's book-derived fantasy life and imaginative paraphernalia was provided from overseas. It was not until later with the *School Journal* and Russell Clark's marvellous art work that I realised stories could exist about New Zealand children doing things I might do in familiar settings. It was a wonderful revelation that books could actually be about *us*.

In my childhood I was spared one now-common influence from overseas because television did not exist here until the 1960s. However, radio's news broadcasts came direct from the BBC in London, and local news was confined to a brief, almost furtive postscript. It certainly created the indelible impression that all really important things happened far away, and what happened nearby was less significant. My grandfather explained, and even now I'm not sure with what accuracy, that the BBC news came via a cable under the sea. I developed a theory that its crackles and fadings were due to the influence of passing fish.

Another constant reminder in my childhood of the variety of the human condition and the natural world – the fascination of far away – was *National Geographic* magazine. Many images from it remain with me to this day. For instance, I remember a photo-story about a group of Burmese women who grew and serrated their fingernails to comb and weave silk for their families' livelihood. They were not only the wives, daughters and mothers of that village but its machinery as well.

I was educated for a time in a Quaker school, and looking back I now think that was very important in the inculcation of values. They taught the virtues of silence and self-reliance, the privilege of knowledge and the joys of reading, the value of quiet time and contemplation. All this was instilled in a remarkably painless way. They taught the self-evident worth of common sense and natural justice in the conduct of human affairs. These two principles seem to me still to be the irreducible standards by which public and private action should be judged, and rejected out of hand if they do not comply. When I presented a radio talk-back show, public outrage was always most intense if common sense and natural justice were felt to have been flouted.

At secondary school most history and literature was British, but geography fascinated me, especially with exotic place names to get your tongue around. A few of the teachers had had overseas experience. The maths mistress was able free-hand to draw a perfect circle on the blackboard and had lived in Latin America but not even that was sufficient to interest me in mathematics. The geography mistress had come from Australia and even that degree of foreignness added greatly to her allure and mystery. In fact I didn't know it in the fourth form, but my first overseas travel was to be to Australia – mainly because I had not saved sufficient money to go further – and I was outraged to discover Melbourne was so large. No one had told me. I was irrationally shocked by the fact. And from my limited experience even Melbourne seemed cosmopolitan. I remember going to a pizza parlour where they flashed words on a screen and you could sing along while you ate your pizza and drank beer. To my youthful self it seemed the height of sophistication, even decadence.

My university studies were fairly haphazard but I was blessed with two splendid literature teachers, Joan Stevens and Vincent O'Sullivan, who made it seem like a great adventure. The university overall did not seem to me a friendly or encouraging place, but those two made knowledge seem infinitely precious and fascinating. They gave you the feeling you could plug into the great traditions of human thought and feeling. With Joan Stevens we studied the modern novel, and that took us all over the world, including to India with E.M. Forster, long before the hippies and ganja-smokers cottoned on to it. What Joan Stevens taught you, indeed embodied, was that there are always other ways of looking at life and the human condition. Vincent O'Sullivan not only taught about literature but wrote it himself. We were in awe of him, but not overawed. When some of us came up with the idea of ringing Robert Graves in Majorca to discuss some point or other he seemed to think this entirely reasonable. In other words, he gave you the idea that knowledge and a concern with literature is an international passport, and that literature always has potential power to bring about personal or political change.

After Victoria University I went high school teaching, but never really felt I had found my vocation therein. One Monday morning with the cooking sherry on the bench and the sixth form essays under the bed I heard an advertisement over 3ZB for auditions for radio announcers. I heard it again on Tuesday morning and on Wednesday morning put two pennies in the

23

phone and made an appointment to be auditioned. Almost in spite of myself I was accepted and a new world opened up. It was the beginning of the rest of my life, I suppose.

The kind of training they gave then was pretty old-fashioned and restricted, but in many ways it has stood me in good stead ever since. They stressed that it was a privilege to enter people's homes on the airwaves, and that like good guests you should never give offence, nor ridicule or make uncomfortable those you were speaking with or to. If you are interviewing, we were told, the listener doesn't want to hear you or your views but those of the person you are interviewing. We were taught that the interviewer was simply to be the conduit to elicit their views. For an interviewer to display personality, or talent, was deemed to be as tasteless as wearing fishnet tights to a christening. All these precepts remain with me as if tattooed into my skin.

Over the years I've interviewed innumerable politicians and public figures, and even if white-knuckled with rage or frustration I've tried to remember that early training. At first Sir Robert Muldoon had what seemed the ultimate put-down. If he didn't want to answer a question he would mockingly remark, 'You've been talking to journalists.' I learned that the way to deal with that or other insults was simply to maintain silence. It works. People can't stand silence and inevitably fill it by saying something. I was amused to read in the *Dictionary of New Zealand Quotations* that the one remark attributed to me was about chairing a discussion between political party leaders at the time of the 1984 election. 'It was,' I said, 'like controlling a playpen full of over-tired toddlers.' Precisely.

My money-managing skills were so deficient that I was in my thirties before I got to Britain and Europe. Of course I loved the history and culture, the architecture and art galleries, drinking wine at café tables and watching the passing parade in Paris. But it did make me realise that there were things you could never afford, levels of intellect you could never match, groups to whom you would never be acceptable and class systems you would never wish to break into. The London I moved in was full of apocryphal stories about New Zealanders who had beaten the system and made good by being oblivious to society's flashing

24

stop-lights. However, the general impression of a smug, closed and classist society made me think more than ever before about New Zealand and New Zealanders. I decided then, and still think, that if you do your mental sums right you feel the accident of being born a New Zealander is fortunate rather than shameful. Our forebears were on average more inquiring, more adventurous, and doubtless had less to lose than the British who stayed behind. If you think about the number of Britons who have migrated all around the world in the last couple of hundred years, it is not surprising that those who remain are the privileged or timid. Later I was to feel much more at ease in the United States of America than ever I did in England.

In mid-career I was lucky enough to be awarded Harkness and Niemann Fellowships which enabled me to study whatever I wanted at Harvard. I'm not sure all my choices were wise but one of the literature courses I most enjoyed was on the myths of American society. It was taught by Sacvan Berkowitz, so named by his mother in memory of the political martyrs Sacco and Vanzetti. He took America's most potent myths of the frontier, of opportunity, progress and freedom and demonstrated that their obverse side was too often genocide, greed, environmental degradation and lawlessness. For him I wrote an essay on the myths of New Zealand, and a singularly difficult assignment I found it too.

When you think about it, our myths are pretty sparse, and in recent times they have taken quite a battering. We were Godzone, but who now believes that? We were a great place to bring up children, but now our infant mortality rates are bettered by Puerto Rico and our media are full of stories of child abuse and domestic violence. We are still supposed to be clean and green but insofar as that is true – and it is debated – it is because we number only three million rather than because we have acted towards our environment with exemplary care and caution. Once our rugby players were invincible but even that is no longer the case. The more I searched for our myths, and for our heroes let alone our heroines, the harder it became to find them. Even our much-vaunted egalitarianism has been eroded, and in any case always had the darker side of levelling down

25

as well as up. The myth of racial harmony was always to some degree wishful thinking, but was at least a better myth to propagate than that of racial superiority. In that essay the lines from Allen Curnow's poem 'Landfall in Unknown Seas' seemed to fit:

Simply by sailing in a new direction
You could enlarge the world.

And I suppose that is the point about both New Zealand and the United States. Both were settled hopefully, as it were, and by people who had fled old rigidities of class, religion or ethnicity. They hoped not to replicate in their new lands the problems of their old.

Following Harvard I spent time working in New York and Washington. In New York I worked inside that arrogant and powerful institution the *New York Times*, and in Washington in that other arrogant and powerful institution, the United States Senate. Both experiences were hugely valuable, though daunting. The *New York Times* took an interest in the *Rainbow Warrior* affair and our anti-nuclear stance. Once when David Lange was passing through I was detailed off to line him up for an interview, but he was not in the mood. They could not believe it. 'Doesn't that asshole realise this is the *New York Times*?' they shrieked. They took themselves very seriously, not only as a journal of record but as a shaper of opinions too. It was awesome to see the resources at their command worldwide, and the way in which they were able to cover crises whenever and wherever they occurred. Working within the *New York Times* gave me splendid insights into how America views the world and, when you think about it, how America views the world shapes all our lives.

In Washington I was an intern on the staff of Senator Simpson from Wyoming. Wyoming in population terms is one of the smallest states, just half a million people, but a very high percentage of them were supporters of Senator Simpson. He wore three separate senatorial hats, so had three separate sets of offices and staff between which he commuted. His main office had bronze statues of cowboys on horseback, and Senator Simpson frequently said he was 'proud' to have nuclear missiles on Wyoming soil. He was 'intrigued' to have me, a New Zealander, on his staff, but made it plain that 'although I don't hold you personally responsible, young lady, New Zealand's anti-nuclear policy is *quite* unacceptable.' Several impressions remain with me from that time: the futility and profligacy of a lot of the work, the desperate self-importance of the aides, and the fiscal laxness. My first pay cheque was supposed to be signed by the senator. When I asked someone to place it on the pile of papers he had to sign when he came in, they said, 'Give it here', and simply forged his signature before my very eyes. With that experience, recent cheque-bouncing scandals within Congress and the Senate surprised me not at all.

In many ways I was sorry to leave America – it had been exhilarating – but coming home with the Fourth Labour Government in power was hardly boring, indeed was perhaps a bit scary at times. I felt frustrated in administrative work, so left the Broadcasting Corporation for print-journalism, but the pull back to radio was very strong and I was delighted to be asked to take over 2ZB morning talk-back. That was an eye-opener, and very good training. You have to get to the point quickly – you don't have the luxury of the more leisurely national radio interviews – and also you feel you are getting in touch with large portions of society with whom you have never had dealings before. There is, of course, a great deal of rage and indignation on talk-back radio, but also sound values about common sense and natural justice, and some lovely humour and warmth. After two years there I was asked to come back to run National Radio's *Nine to Noon* programme and that has felt like another homecoming.

I am not simply interested in eliciting facts, but highlighting the significance of those facts. My job is to interest people in what is going on in their own society, and in the wider world. In the course of this you can only hope new ideas make people more tolerant and more aware of points of view other than their own. Distance is not the deterrent it once was. I can and do ring round the world for eye-witness accounts and expert commentary. I also have the luxury of choosing what to focus on, and often those can be life-enhancing things such as the arts or books.

One development in recent years that seems to me to be exciting and worthwhile is the flourishing of local publishers and the proliferation of New Zealand books. Just look at each year's nominations for the New Zealand Book Awards and the Goodman Fielder Wattie Awards. Wonderful reference books such as *The Dictionary of New Zealand Biography* and *The Book of New Zealand Women* have revealed great swathes of the past we scarcely knew existed, and many new volumes each year examine our politics, our social concerns, our public life. Fiction writers, too, contribute to our national myths. Two of the most powerful recent novels, Keri Hulme's *the bone people* and Alan Duff's *Once Were Warriors*, disturb by their depiction of violence but one dare not doubt their truths. Happily the poets have been rather more celebratory in contributing to our sense of self and self-esteem.

We are frequently an ambivalent people and not for nothing is 'the great New Zealand clobbering machine' a part of our collective mental baggage. Once again I found in Curnow this insight about the New Zealander:

> Wholehearted he cannot move
> From where he is, nor love
> Wholeheartedly that place. . . .
> ('The Eye Is More or Less Satisfied with Seeing')

I should like in my work to contribute to a sense of wholeheartedness about New Zealand. We have so many blessings to count and so much to feel joyous about. I'm no Pollyanna, but living elsewhere has highlighted for me what is good about this place. We make good things. We have a sophisticated infrastructure. Our cities are still manageable. There remains some kindness in the state and much decency in society. We teach girls to read and write and we buy and borrow more books per capita than any other country. We have left religious bigotry behind us. Somewhat hesitatingly, some of us grumbling, we have grasped the nettle of biculturalism and know there is no turning back. We have easy access to beaches, lakes, the countryside. We eat and drink well. The arts flourish. The rugby, racing and beer national myth will simply no longer do.

# A Bit of an Escapade

## Christopher Doig

I am afraid I was a pretty typical New Zealander in that I was fanatical about sport and fairly intolerant of the finer things in life. Music, however, was inescapable in that my mother came from a strongly Methodist background and singing was always part of the family tradition. Each Sunday morning we would sing in the church choir, then come home and gather round the piano to sing in four-part harmony. My grandfather had a particularly fine voice, my aunt was a trained singer, and my mother, a fine singer herself, would accompany us all on the piano. I just loved it, but would have died rather than admit it at the time.

When I went to Christchurch Boys' High School the height of my ambition was to make the first cricket and hockey elevens. However, as well as a strong sporting tradition the school was noted for its music, and willy-nilly all third formers were auditioned for one or other of the school choirs. I was fairly phlegmatic about getting into the treble choir, but by the time I got to the fifth form I was on the way to achieving my sporting ambitions and was determined not to succeed in getting into the main school choir. I deliberately tried to mess up the audition and to sing badly, but the music master was having none of that, and I was mortified not only to be dragooned into the choir but to be sorted out as a potential school soloist as well.

That music master, Clifton Cook, was a remarkable man, and next to Sister Mary Leo he was probably the most notable singing teacher in New Zealand. In fact he produced more successful international singers – Richard Greager, Anson Austin, Edmund Bowen, Elric Hooper, Kerry Henderson, Andrew Dalley – than anyone else I know. He had the facility to free the natural voice, to instil in his pupils a relatively mature sound, and to give you an absolute love of what you were doing.

At the beginning, however, I was singularly ungrateful for his attentions. I remember going home to my parents and loudly complaining that Cook was off his rocker in that he thought I should have private singing lessons with him. My somewhat older and wiser brother John, who is now a leading Christchurch gynaecologist, said quietly that he had always wanted to sing properly, so if I weren't man enough to have lessons by myself he would come along with me – and he did. I swore him to absolute secrecy as singing lessons didn't fit in with the macho sporting identity I still sought to project.

Clifton Cook, I'll never forget it, began that first lesson by saying 'Doig, if you do what I tell you, this will change your life.' It was not at all what I wanted to hear. His next pronouncement I wanted to hear even less: 'The school concert is in the Civic Theatre in three weeks' time and you will sing solo.' These concerts were basically a display of the school's musical wares – the orchestra, the band, the various choirs and one or two soloists. The Civic Theatre was packed with 1500 adoring parents and I was absolutely petrified, but that was my first solo performance, at the age of sixteen.

I studied as a baritone with Clifton until my second year at university, where I did an honours degree in English and French. I sang with the university choir and the Christchurch Harmonic Choir, did some solo, radio and competition work, but I still had senior cricket and hockey commitments as my first priority. At that stage I had my first and most serious row with Clifton as I said I simply did not *want* to be a professional singer, and I did not *like* the kind of pressure to which he was subjecting me. I stopped lessons for two years, but took them up again when, after graduation, I moved to Auckland to go to teachers' college and to pursue the lady who became my first wife. I then resumed private lessons with Philip Todd, who was the vocal tutor at Auckland University.

It was in Auckland that I had my first real professional engagement in the Benjamin Britten opera, *The Burning Fiery Furnace*. In fact Britten and Peter Pears came out to New Zealand for it, and made an enormous impression on me. The principal singer was the New Zealander, Brian Drake. I saw quite a bit of Britten and Pears socially, felt very impressed with the whole scene, and I began to think that maybe singing for a living might not be such a bad idea after all.

In 1972 I entered the Mobil Song Quest. By that stage I was teaching English and French at Auckland Grammar (I had nothing to do with the musical life of the school but coached many of the senior sports teams). I got into the last twelve contestants and before going to Christchurch for the final took advice from the previous year's winner. She reminded me that it was still a radio contest. The judge was sitting in a studio outside the hall. So her advice was to ignore the audience, to concentrate on the microphone and to sing within myself, thus refining the sound. That is what I did. I sang to the microphone and it worked. I won.

On the flight home to Auckland I overheard one of the unsuccessful competitors complaining that the prize was wasted on me, as my wife and I were likely to use the money to carpet our new house. As the prize was a mere $1000 the suggestion was pretty unrealistic, but the remark served to enrage me and I decided there and then to take leave of absence from my job and to study singing overseas.

The then headmaster of Auckland Grammar, Henry Cooper, was supportive, my flautist wife was supportive, and the Queen Elizabeth II Arts Council was supportive in the most practical way and gave me a grant of $1500. I loved school teaching and thought of this really as a bit of an escapade, as a two year interruption to my real career. We would get a bit of Overseas Experience then come back and 'settle down'.

The 'normal' thing for young New Zealand singers to do was to go to London for further training. I wanted to be different, and to concentrate on German Lied singing. By happy coincidence, a reputable Austrian composer, Professor Robert Schollum of the Vienna Hochschule, visited New Zealand at this time. He heard me sing, and when he went home facilitated my entry to the Hochschule, which was the major academy in Vienna.

My wife and two young children and I arrived in Vienna in January 1975. It was freezing, we had very little German between us, we knew absolutely no one, and our life savings including the Arts Council grant amounted to $5000. You have to be young to embark on such a perilous enterprise. When I went to audition at the Hochschule they said, 'Mr Doig, we think you have a fine voice, but we think you are a tenor.' I replied that I was pretty nonchalant about that, so long as it didn't involve any drastic surgery.

I enjoyed studying German Lieder with Robert Schollum, but my first vocal coach was a bit of a disaster. She agreed with the judgement that I was a tenor, but instead of easing me into that new and higher range repertoire, she booted me into some fearsomely difficult arias, and the voice began to deteriorate badly. It was my very good fortune that Clifton Cook came to visit at that time. He was on a world tour looking up former violin, organ, piano and singing pupils. He had them scattered everywhere, and continued to take a lively interest in their progress long after they passed from his care. He listened to me glumly, and thought I had gone backwards rather than forwards. He said he thought the voice had lost what it once had. He set about doing a bit of detective work by talking to the wife of one of the members of the Prague Quartet in Vienna whom he had befriended years before in Christchurch. He came back with the verdict that I should be studying with Professor Anton Dermota who, along with Fritz Wunderlich, was the greatest lyric tenor in post-war Austria. The Prague Quartet miraculously arranged for him to audition me, an obscure young New Zealander. Without Clifton Cook's intervention I would never even have got into the great man's presence.

Wonder of wonders, he agreed to teach me repertoire, but said I would also need a vocal coach. He was very professional about not denigrating or criticising my existing vocal coach, but said I should listen around to find the kind of sound I would like to achieve. I discovered that all the students whose voices I most admired were studying with the same teacher, Alexander Kolo. He agreed to train me as a tenor, and even more remarkably he offered to do it free. This was a real godsend as we were rapidly eroding our tiny capital. The condition on which he agreed to take me was that I would give up all existing repertoire and devote six months entirely to vocal exercises. It was dementia-making, but it worked dramatically. Within a month I had hugely enlarged the range of my voice, and was singing high Cs when previously I had been unable to go above G. Within six months I was physically a fully fledged tenor, but it took much longer than that emotionally and psychologically to accept the quite different range and demands of singing as a tenor.

My first break-through in the tenor repertoire came with a second placing in the prestigious Hugo Wolf Competition in Salzburg in 1976. There were singers competing from all round the world, and I guarantee that if I weren't the youngest, I was certainly the *newest* tenor. It was quite reassuring that the change was proving worthwhile and successful.

Our two years in Vienna were very hard financially, and prospective students should be warned. Rents are high and 'key money' exorbitant by New Zealand standards. Before leaving Auckland for Vienna I had organised a job for myself at the American School to supplement family income, but when I arrived the headmaster had been transferred and no job existed. My wife and I traipsed the streets prepared to do absolutely anything – clean floors, sell newspapers or whatever – but in Austria if you are university educated or qualified they will not employ you in menial jobs because they would be obligated to pay too much. After six months we were broke and wrote home to parents asking for return airfares as we could see no way of staying on. Interestingly, that 'begging' letter apparently never arrived, but what did miraculously appear was a further $5000 from the Arts Council.

Our salvation had been wrought, I understand, by an old hockey-playing friend of mine, renal surgeon Ross Bailey, who had visited us and could see we were having a hard time. Apparently, when he got back to New Zealand he got in touch with

John Ritchie, who had awarded me first prize in the Mobil Song Quest, and on his own initiative he had arranged for the Arts Council to send the cheque that reprieved us. Later I was able to get work at the Berlitz Institute teaching English, but without that $5000 we wouldn't have been able to carry on. I remain deeply indebted to both John Ritchie and the Arts Council.

Vienna, however, was not unmitigated hard work and drudgery. We were regular and delighted patrons of the Vienna State Opera. My wife and I went on alternate nights as often as we could. One of us had to babysit. Standing room cost just one Austrian schilling for students – it cost more to go to the toilet once you were there – and we hugely stretched our knowledge and love of the opera repertoire. Soloists flew in from round the world and their magic obliterated the discomfort of standing. The Academy too had been rewarding and accommodating. I had had to compress something like a five-year course into two years, and they had bent over backwards to be helpful in bringing forward final exams and suchlike. I graduated with distinction after only two years in 1976.

So the time drew near for us to go back to New Zealand, but Anton Dermota intervened to suggest to the Vienna State Opera that they should audition me. I went along in a wonderful frame of mind. On the one hand I was overwhelmed at just standing on the stage of that magnificent opera house, and on the other I didn't give a damn about the audition's outcome because I loved teaching, loved New Zealand and had a very good job to return to. They were not much impressed with my Puccini aria – my voice was too light at that stage – but they did like my Mozart and offered me a contract on the spot. To their astonishment I said I did not think I wanted it, but they were kind enough to say they would leave the offer open in case I changed my mind once I got back to New Zealand.

In Auckland I went practically straight from the plane to the Grammar School as it was February and term had begun. I had loved that school, its academic excellence and its emphasis on all-round development. I had felt privileged to teach there and looked forward to getting back into my stride. On that first morning there was a staff meeting, and to my astonishment sixty or so accomplished adults sat round debating the cost of tea and biscuits for the year. I could not believe it and went straight to John Graham, the then headmaster, and said I wanted to resign and return to Vienna. We were very good friends, and he was horrified that I was contemplating what he saw as a rootless life. He persuaded me against resigning, but instead extended my leave of absence another two years. To finance our journey we perhaps unwisely sold our house, and returned to Vienna in August.

Back in Vienna I was attached initially to what was called the Studio, with other promising young singers. It was in a way a cheap labour pool for the Opera House, for we were treated exactly the same as fully fledged professionals, only not paid nearly as much. I was very inexperienced and was really just thrown in at the deep end. The Vienna State Opera orchestra and chorus know their repertoire and the productions backwards, experienced principals are flown in from all over the world just a day or so before any performance, and rehearsals are minimal for repertoire pieces because everyone is expected to know what they are doing.

My debut was horrifying. The part was not large – Guiseppe in *La Traviata* – and I was musically sound with it. However, I turned up to the one and only rehearsal to find it had been cancelled because an airline strike had prevented the arrival of two of the principals from Italy. So all that happened was that an assistant stage manager showed me photos of the sets, described my actions, and that was that. On the night, I was costumed and made up and the conductor came to tell me how he wanted me to react and what speed he proposed – at least that is the sort of thing I presumed he was telling me, for it was all in fluent Italian, none of which I understood at that time. I then found myself alone, the opera had started, and I realised I had no idea where the stage was in relation to my dressing room. Someone rescued me and flung me on stage at the appropriate point. I was to sing a small aria and deliver a letter to the lead tenor, but he wasn't where he was supposed to be, as he had not been rehearsed either. It was, you might say, a learning experience. Whatever they asked me to do I said I could. It was the New

Zealand 'can do' mentality coming through, I suppose. Anyway it paid off. They recognised my willingness and rewarded me with many performances. The contract said that after thirty performances I would be paid a performance fee for each subsequent one, and it took me not much more than three months to get the thirty under my belt.

At this time Kiri Te Kanawa came to Vienna to record Richard Strauss's *Four Last Songs*. We had known of each other in Auckland, as we both worked with a very fine pianist, Barbara Brown. When she returned to London she very kindly arranged for me to have an audition with Covent Garden. My Vienna agent then arranged for me also to audition at Basel on the way to London. Straight away I was offered a full contract with Basel and two guest contracts with Covent Garden. I asked for leave to do the guest contracts with Covent Garden and was pretty annoyed when the Vienna State Opera would not give me permission. So I told them I would go full time to Basel, and they said they would match this offer and give me a full permanent contract in Vienna.

The children were settled, the Vienna State Opera was enormously prestigious, and I was flattered. We decided to stay, but in retrospect that was probably a mistake. Admittedly I got to do something like forty different roles over the next four years; I worked with wonderful singers, directors and conductors, and I was well paid. But had I gone to Basel I would have had lead roles, we would have rehearsed thoroughly on fewer productions, it probably would have been a less hectic professional life and better training, and it would have allowed me to develop as an artist. However, Vienna had real compensations and I did get fully integrated into the wider musical life of the city. For instance, I did several Lieder concerts and oratorios with artists like Peter Schreier and Hermann Prey, and several agents began taking notice. My major agent suggested it was time to move from the Vienna State Opera to another house where I could take lead rather than secondary roles, learn my craft thoroughly and develop my technique. So as not to disrupt the children and my concert career, I auditioned for the nearest opera house, Linz. I sang a huge number of roles in Linz for four years, then auditioned for the position of lead lyric tenor at a bigger house in Kassel, West Germany, with a view to returning to the Vienna State Opera after this contract. Fate intervened, however, and I never took up that job.

In January of 1984 the Munich State Opera asked me to go to La Scala with them in a production of *Ariadne auf Naxos*. I was very excited because it was a marvellous cast, and to sing at La Scala is like playing at Lords if you are a cricketer. Our engagement was for six weeks and for the first time I had the experience of living in close proximity with stars, unlike Vienna where they flew in for a few days only. I enjoyed the experience but it also made me uneasy. I found that they lived with massive personal pressure. If they did not get a standing ovation every single night they began to worry that their voice was fading. Most of them, too, had pretty strained personal lives, with failed marriages and things like that. The husband of one of them had just committed suicide because the star had gone off with a young Viennese. It was pretty horrendous and at the back of my mind I began wondering if I really wanted to live like this all my life.

During the last fortnight of my contract with Linz I got news that my father was dying. To my horror they would not give me leave of absence to visit him. I got a sympathetic doctor to write that I was not fit to fulfil the last two weeks of my contract, and flew back to New Zealand for the first time in eight years. Despite the sad circumstances of my return, I simply fell in love with the place again. I remember playing golf with Martin Hadlee and saying that New Zealanders seemed not to realise how lucky they were, and that I would give anything to be able to live here again. I couldn't, however, see any future professionally as an opera singer in New Zealand at that time, and said that returning to the bottom of the pile as a teacher daunted me. I was talking to the right man. Martin was secretary/treasurer of the Christchurch Arts Centre and their director had just resigned. Would I be interested in the job? The board and I met on the very next day and they made an offer on the spot.

My wife and the children were visiting her family in Auckland so I flew up to discuss the possibility of change to all our lives. We sat around in a friend's spa pool debating the pros and cons, and I got out of that pool having decided I was a New Zealander first and foremost, and singing wasn't the be-all and end-all of my existence. I decided, too, that I wanted my children to be New Zealanders and to enjoy the advantages we had had growing up here. I had developed a real aversion to the education system in Austria. Their schools are like office buildings and have no play-grounds. The discipline is fierce and there are no opportunities for creativity or exuberance. On one occasion we were summoned because our son Paul had run down the school corridor in the interval. We explained to him that running round was *verboten* and gave him a book to read during the break between classes. We were summoned again and told that that was not allowed either! The pressure for examination success from an early age was extraordinary too. We were solemnly advised by a teacher that we should tranquillise our ten-year-old daughter before exams as her nervousness meant she did not perform to expecta-tions, especially in maths. I could not believe it but they meant it. The regimentation at every level of Austrian schools had to be experienced to be believed, and I decided I wanted my children to have the open, free and uncomplicated learning environment we had enjoyed and thrived in. So we came back.

Arriving in Christchurch I felt instantly at home. Boyhood friends were still there and there was exactly the same friendly ease and openness there had always been. The Christchurch Arts Centre was housed in the old central campus of the University of Canterbury where I had fallen in love with language and lit-erature, so that was a kind of homecoming too. I loved the job and hope I did it well. One of the things we got going in the four years I was there was the Canterbury Opera with a wonderful production of *The Magic Flute*. It was a huge success, even finan-cially, and it got my singing career going again. Unbeknown to me, in the audience one night was the London-based agent, Haydn Rawstron. He said nothing to me about my performance but rang later from Australia to ask whether I was interested in auditioning for the tenor lead in a bicentenary production of *The Coronation of Poppea* with the Australian Opera. I got the role, was simultaneously taken on by the Australian agent, Jenifer Eddy, and things have gone from strength to strength since then.

I have a permanent guest contract with the Australian Opera and spend about six months of the year there, which I love.

After four years in Christchurch I was approached by Sir David Beattie to see if I would like to take over as director of the Wellington-based International Festival of the Arts. It was a good time to move, as my marriage had broken up. My four years in Wellington were hugely busy, but also enormously satisfying. The Festival now has a life of its own and is, I hope, a permanent and exciting part of New Zealand life.

Meanwhile I am being inundated with opera singing offers. The Australian opera houses often import distinguished international conductors and directors, and I now have the ironic situation where I live back in New Zealand but am being offered more and better roles in Europe than when I lived there: the Welsh National Opera, Stuttgart, Hamburg, Cologne and other opera houses. I have a lot of travelling in the pipeline. It is a matter of age, maturity and experience, of course. I am technically better now than ever before, and also I am singing a repertoire that very few people do. It has opened up new opportunities and I am enjoying them all. The greatest advantage is that with modern air travel I can do it all from my New Zealand base. Even now when I set foot in Frankfurt I cannot wait to get back here. There are a growing number of internationally distinguished New Zealand opera singers who now live here and commute to the opposite side of the world. Looking back, I was happy enough in Austria but always felt exiled in some profound sense.

My new wife, Dunedin-born Suzanne Prain, is an opera singer who is pursuing her career internationally from our Christchurch base. The next ten or fifteen years will, with a bit of luck, be internationally active, but we have the good fortune of knowing we have a home we can always come to, and a place where we belong. New Zealand per capita has produced an extraordinary number of successful opera singers. Perhaps music and singing will come one day to be seen as just as worthy of approbation and emulation in our national life and national self-image as is sport. Perhaps the next generation will not need to feel so fearful of musical talent and commitment as I was.

# I Feel at Home with My Work Being Here

## John Drawbridge

It wasn't until about 1939 that I first became vaguely aware of lands beyond our shores. I remember then that my big disappointment was that the Coldstream Guards Band was not coming to the Centennial Exhibition in Wellington, because of the declaration of war.

Soon fathers, uncles and cousins went away and later we were invaded by American Marines. Women teachers took over boys' secondary schools. Most of them were very good teachers and they brought another dimension to the 'macho' boys' schools of that time. Throughout the early 1940s there were ageing men and younger women teaching all over the country. In those days I used to go to Saturday morning art classes at the old Technical College, because there was no proper art teacher at our school. The man in charge of art at our school was a maths teacher and he would grill me each Monday morning to find out what I had done at the Saturday art class. Whatever I had done would be given to the school's art classes for the whole of the next week. Therefore, whether I liked it or not I had to go to the Technical College every Saturday without fail.

I remember, too, when I was in the third form, an inspector came into the class one day, looked over my shoulder at the painting I was doing, and said 'Picassio'! I couldn't find any information on Picassio, or did he mean Pissarro? So when I eventually found a few reproductions of Picasso and of Pissarro I realised that inspectors who were supposed to know everything did not, in fact, know much about art. The painting I was working on, although 'modern art', was not remotely like a Picasso. Later, in 1948, I bought my first big art book, *Picasso, Fifty Years of His Art*, by Alfred H. Barr. I got to know this book and the paintings in it so well that when I visited the Museum of Modern Art in New York in the early 1960s, Picasso's painting of 'A Girl Before a Mirror' gave me the feeling that I had actually painted it years before.

There were very few art books available until some years after the war. Then Penguin brought out the wonderful series, *Modern Painters*. Because Frances Hodgkins was included in it, it in some ways made artists in New Zealand think we had really 'made it'. Just as writers looked to Katherine Mansfield, perhaps painters felt that they were made part of the wider art world with the overseas acclaim of Frances Hodgkins. We were not only naive and inexperienced, but also, though unavoidably, incredibly ignorant. I remember the locally well-known artist, Sam Cairncross, emerging from the public library, exclaiming, 'This chap Van Gogh paints just like me!'

There were no dealer galleries in Wellington until the late 1940s, when Helen Hitchings opened a remarkable gallery upstairs in an old warehouse in Bond Street. The National Art Gallery and Museum had been moved out of its building during the war so that the Air Force could move in there. Goodness knows what they were trying to protect! Even so, the National Gallery moved a small part of their collection to the tea-rooms of the D.I.C. building in Lambton Quay, where they held some memorable small exhibitions in this mid-city space. Kirkcaldie and Stains also had a big room which they would use from time to time for large temporary exhibitions. Wellington Central Public Library had charging exhibitions and were the first to show a big exhibition of Colin McCahon's paintings. The French Maid coffee shop was a meeting place for conversation and also had small exhibitions on a regular basis. At about this time the publication by Harry H. Toombs of the *New Zealand Arts Yearbook* under the editorship of Howard Wadman and then Eric Lee-Johnson was an important event, rather like the *Boys' Own Annual*.

After the war things were on the move in education and particularly in art education under the enlightened leadership of Dr C.E. Beeby and his extraordinary staff. In specialist areas, people such as Gordon Tovey in art, Philip Smithells in physical education and Cliff O'Malley as art editor of School Publications were inspirational to both teachers and students. My parents were always tolerant of my early paintings and later they were encouraging, even though my father was particularly anxious about my future. I think he thought that my skills of manipulation could be turned to good use, and profit, if I were to become a dentist!

When I left secondary school I spent a year at the Wellington Technical College Art School. Most of the staff under the head of school, Fred Ellis, had been trained at the Royal College of Art in London. They were genuine, concerned teachers, even if they were somewhat frustrated artists. I think that many of them thought that they were following Gauguin's footsteps to the romance of a Pacific paradise. This small, intimate art school was a kind of prep-school for the university schools of fine art. The training was pseudo-academic and rather dull, and it put me off the idea of further study in art schools. I was fearful of what I then considered to be the imposition of some of the teachers' attitudes on top of my own work, and it seemed to me then that the most interesting painting was going on outside the environs of academic training. It didn't occur to me that I was arrogant, but I was probably pig-headed about what I felt I wanted to learn. I doubt that I actually intellectualised my feelings in this way at that time.

However, in 1949 I decided to go to Wellington Teachers' Training College. The teachers' colleges, and to a certain extent the universities, were awakening to the values of creative work in writing, music and art. Wellington Teachers' College, under the gentle guidance of Reg Waghorn, had an extraordinary staff, and there were also a number of older, war rehabilitation students.

Until I went to the teachers' college I did not realise that my secondary education had been so incomplete. I had not even heard of the contemporary writing of T.S. Eliot, George Orwell or Frank Sargeson. Walter Scott, Patrick Macaskill and Anton Vogt soon made up for what I had previously missed. Tom

Young not only taught me to appreciate the abstract beauty of music, but he also introduced me to the abstract paintings of Kandinsky. Arthur Barker, the science lecturer, was not just a scientist; he was a translator of Rimbaud's poetry and also an excellent knitter. What it meant most of all was that these people were not only 'subject' lecturers but that they were 'real' people. Louise Henderson was one of this remarkable group. At the age of eighteen, I think the biggest lesson I learnt was with the death of our art lecturer, Roland Hipkins. Here I was, training to be a teacher, and I remember Hipkins saying to me the day before he died that he was looking forward to retirement so that he could paint. Roland Hipkins' death made me determined not to be 'swallowed up' by the demands of teaching – nor to wait until later to paint.

With Barry Mitcalfe, John Ford, Judith Alley, Jeanne Benseman and many others, the Glencoe Publishing Company was created in the old tennis pavilion in The Glen at Kelburn. This enabled the young writers to get into print. John Thomson, who was at Victoria University at that time, established first *Hilltop* and then later *Arachne*, with young writers, such as Alistair Campbell and James K. Baxter, as well as other artists and intellectuals all contributing. This surge of creativity could well have been a world-wide phenomenon after the war. It was happening here in New Zealand and we were vaguely aware of what was going on overseas also.

*Landfall*, through Charles Brasch, and *Design Review*, from the Architectural Centre, were starting to give us some idea of ourselves. The National Film Unit, too, was changing from a propaganda machine into an organisation capable of taking a closer look at ourselves, with Brian Brake being its youngest and most innovative film maker.

The arrival, before and after the war, of a few Jewish and European immigrés made a difference; they made discerning demands of performance in music, and they also gave some recognition to our more original artists. Mario and Hilda Fleischl were amongst the few who collected paintings by McCahon, Woollaston and Theo Schoon, and they encouraged Douglas Lilburn. Ernst Plischke made architecture into a contemporary art form and he was highly respected by the young architects, many of whom were the original members of the Architectural Centre. But generally speaking the home-grown populace was neither moved by nor remotely interested in any of this.

With Helen Hitchings's encouragement, my first exhibition was held in her gallery in 1949. Other artists exhibiting paintings in Helen's gallery were Keith Patterson, George Johnson and Douglas MacDiarmid. Later, at the Architectural Centre Gallery, Don Peebles, Vic Gray, John Pine Snadden, Melvin Day, Pat Hanly, Bill Culbert and Brian Carmody became the vanguard of new painting of the 1950s. In time we would all leave New Zealand and most of us would eventually return.

Before the days of the QEII Arts Council, for painters there were the annual awards from the National Art Gallery and the Association of New Zealand Art Societies. These travelling scholarships were entirely worthwhile as they recognised the need for prolonged study overseas. Paul Olds, Michael Brown and Tom Coomber had been awarded the National Art Gallery travelling scholarship before Bill Culbert and I both received it at the same time in 1957. The scholarship was awarded to each artist for three years' overseas study, mine at the Central School of Art and Craft in London.

I was twenty-six years old. Before this I had spent a few years as an art adviser with a great team of teachers under Gordon Tovey's guidance. Then, for a while, I was fortunate to teach with Doreen Blumhardt on the staff at Wellington Teachers' College. People kept leaving New Zealand to study, to work or perhaps to follow in the footsteps of Frances Hodgkins' fame. In those days few people flew, and the trip abroad was something to look forward to and prepare for with longing anticipation. It was not really until the late 1960s that people began to accept flying as the way to come and go. This relative ease of departure changed the whole aspect of New Zealanders' feelings of our place in the world. Travel by air does not have the same strong emotional impact as sea travel. The size, the space of the great oceans, the places of arrival on the way . . . Pitcairn, Panama and Curaçao were the first places to set foot on after leaving New Zealand, and it was a most extraordinary experience. Is the rest of the world like Panama City?, you wondered.

I travelled to London with Brian Carmody and it was enriching to share experiences with another artist. We looked, and sketched together in such places as the back streets of Curaçao. When I arrived in London, my first visits, often with Brian, were to the Tate Gallery and to the National Gallery. Surprisingly, it took me a long time to get used to looking at original paintings. After all, I had grown up on reproductions of paintings in books and my first reaction to the originals was sometimes one of disappointment. At the same time, however, I was often overwhelmed by my experiences of original paintings. Eventually the reproductions I had known became mere reminders of the real thing. Actual size, colour and technique, I realised, could never be reproduced in books. In England, too, the resurgence of printmaking through the influence of S.W. Hayter had hit British artists and the art schools. I had not seen anything like these works in New Zealand and they were a shock to me. They were large and colourful original artists' prints.

It was then that I also met some real artists – people who lived for their work. Not only were they famous artists but some were my teachers at the Central School in London. The principal there was William Johnson. He was an enlightened art educator with innovative ideas. One of his ideas was to use artists as part-time teachers in areas of work outside their own disciplines. There were many different departments at the school, and Johnson would employ people such as Eduardo Paolozzi, who was a well-known sculptor, in the Department of Textile Design. Gordon Crook was also on the staff at the Central School, and at that time there was no hint that eventually he would come to New Zealand to live.

The most important teachers for me in London were Merlyn Evans in etching, and Mervyn Peake, the great writer, who taught me life drawing. In the print workshop Evans was inspirational. He was an artist with a profound philosophy and his personal discussions with students made us feel not just worthwhile, but important. Evans was free to discuss ideas of art and life because he had the advantage of having technicians in the workshop, whose job it was to teach and help with the technicalities of printmaking.

Sharing experiences was also achieved by having students of all ages and backgrounds of experience working together in the same rooms. It was here that I first met Robert MacDonald, a journalist, painter and printmaker from New Zealand. Kathan Brown from the USA was part of this group. Later she was to establish the now famous Crown Point Press in California.

The other great thing about living and working in London at that time was that there were artists and students from all over the world. Their influences on me and upon each other were of great value. At the Central School, students from many different countries worked in their own disciplines at a very high level of accomplishment. There were mural painters, illustrators, graphic designers, textile designers, theatre designers, industrial designers, interior and furniture designers, silversmiths, bookbinders, stained-glass artists, printmakers and painters. It was at the Central School that I first met Tanya Ashken, who was doing the silversmiths' course there.

In the summer of 1958, Brian Carmody, Marion Rayward and I spent three months travelling and sketching around Europe. Drawing has helped me, and I'm sure Brian too, to recall vividly the places and events we visited. I'm sure that we could now, so many years later, go back to the exact places we sketched.

It's hard to talk about in one breath, as it were, but seeing the masterpieces in the Louvre, the Prado, Uffizi and the Rijksmuseum had, I think, one strange advantage for us. We had not grown up with these works and in some ways we were not intimidated by the traditions surrounding them. Ancient cities, cathedrals, churches, paintings, sculpture, and people and language were all new and strange to us. It was as though we were new arrivals, re-born, or alien visitors from 'outer space'.

Gradually, as I became more and more familiar with some of the great paintings from the past, an extraordinary thing began to happen to me. The people in the streets of Florence looked as though they had walked straight off the walls of the chapel of Santa Maria Del Carmine, which Masaccio had painted in the fifteenth century. Street fights at night, and the police in Madrid, were from Goya's paintings. And it seemed that the peasants in Europe all came from Brueghel, Millet and Van Gogh. The landscape too was from Cézanne in the south of France, and further south it was Matisse and Bonnard. The more I got to know of the landscape, the people and the events, the more I saw them through the artists' eyes and minds. The strong feeling I had was that whatever I looked at had been looked at millions of times, by millions of eyes, for hundreds of years. It was a different sense I had about places and things seen and lived with, growing up in New Zealand. This all tended to emphasise for me the loneliness of McCahon, Frank Sargeson and Douglas Lilburn in New Zealand.

In 1960 Tanya Ashken and I were married and it was with good fortune that the National Art Gallery awarded me a fourth year on my travelling scholarship. Tanya and I had finished our courses at the Central School and we left London to study and work for a year in Paris. Tanya decided to work in sculpture, stone carving in the atelier of an Italian called del Debbio. His studio was in a cluster of artists' studios and workshops – Brancusi, Tinguely and Lacasse had their studios there. These studios and the nearby cafés were still great meeting places for artists. As well as painting, I continued to do printmaking, firstly in S.W. Hayter's atelier and then at Johnny Friedlaender's. The way of studying in Paris was to work alongside others privileged enough to work in the master's studio.

Arriving in Paris from London was rather like arriving in London from Wellington. Whilst I was overwhelmed by Old Master paintings I was constantly coming across exhibitions of paintings by contemporary artists I had never heard of before. Giacometti, Dubuffet, Viera Da Silva and many others were famous in Europe but were unknown to me. Even now the paintings of unknown artists are often a positive discovery for me – discoveries which are often unexpected and expansive. But mostly, there is always a huge amount of bad contemporary work which never moves me. One of the good things about living so close to Old and Modern Masters in public galleries was that I could return time and time again to see my favourite Rembrandts, Cézannes and Picassos. Each time I went to see the same painting I would see something in it I had never seen before. The depth of such experience was magical. It was like re-

reading a good book at different times in my life. As with books, paintings stay the same, but my understanding of them changes, and continues to change. The familiar often contains an essence of new experience for me. This response was by no means confined to modern paintings – it applied even more to my discovery of Paolo Uccello and Piero Della Francesca. Turner, Constable and Monet also never failed to move me.

My favourite place in London, which I continued to return to for years, was the Print Room at the British Museum. Here I was able to look at Goya's and Rembrandt's etchings on my own. The intimacy of their etchings made me feel that these artists were speaking directly to me. It was here that I also discovered the etchings of Dunoyer de Segonzac, Jacques Villon and Giorgio Morandi. Later I was honoured when the British Museum and the Victoria and Albert Museum bought prints of mine.

When we lived in Paris one of my favourite places was Lacourière's workshop, where I would watch expert printers printing the etchings of Picasso, Chagall and Braque. In Europe the tradition had always been for the well-known artists to produce their original works on the copper plates or on the lithographic stone, and for the master printers to print editions under the artists' supervision. Lacourière's workshop was on the hill of Montmartre high above Paris and just below the Basilique du Sacré-Coeur. Paris was dotted with small workshops of different kinds. We lived on the Left Bank, near the Jardin du Luxembourg and close to the 'Mouleur' or plaster modeller for Hans Arp. Foreign artists would often live in tiny rooms in cheap hotels, and they would meet and work in the studios of the Paris-based artists. What was so good and encouraging was that these artists were usually interested in what others were doing. And the Rue de Seine, Rue Bonaparte, Rue des Beaux Arts and the Boulevard Saint Germain were full of small dealer galleries, bookshops, antique shops and cafés. In the early 1960s Paris was always full of armed police because of the continuing problems between France and Algeria. I could never believe that I would get used to revolvers, guns, plastic bombs and demonstrations.

The London dealers loved coming to Paris. I had already had some success in London with the Leicester Gallery and the Piccadilly Gallery before we had left for Paris, and the dealers from these galleries would turn up from time to time and send my paintings back to London to exhibit and sell. The French galleries were never keen to exhibit works by English-speaking people, unless they were Scots. I could only show the occasional print in Paris. No matter how good you were, it was difficult to show paintings as the dealers always had their own 'stable' of artists. It was much the same in London too.

But in Paris, French artists are treasured people. Tanya and I were in Paris when Georges Braque died in 1963, and the whole of France mourned his passing. In England, or New Zealand, it makes little difference to anyone unless a politician dies. Even when Rita Angus and McCahon died, the reaction tended to be about the increased monetary value of their work. This was not acclaim of the artists as much as it was a stockbroker's or auctioneer's view of investment. The death of Braque, McCahon and all considerable artists, writers and composers always marks the end of an era.

When Tanya and I returned to live in London I felt like a person without a language. After more than a year in France I didn't know the language very well, but I had almost forgotten how to think and speak in English! I had to find a job and we also had to find somewhere to live. For a year I taught in a boys' comprehensive school in the East End. The community were largely established Jewish families and new West Indian and African families. There was often conflict amongst the young people at this school and fights and knives were not uncommon. In some respects trying to teach art was a pointless exercise. It was a shock to me to come from doing my own work and study in Paris to face this very different reality. In the end I am sure that I learnt very much more from these boys than they ever learnt from me.

After working in the East End I was fortunate to get a part-time job at Isleworth Polytechnic, teaching drawing and painting to tertiary students. Being a part-time job, this gave me much more time and energy to continue with my own work. At the heart of modern buildings at Isleworth Polytechnic was the old mansion of Joseph Banks. It was an extraordinary time lapse for me, that I should teach drawing in the Banksian Room – a large conservatory full of New Zealand and Pacific Island plants still growing there.

At about this time Robert Matthew, the architect, invited me to submit ideas to him for a large mural for the reception hall for the new New Zealand House being built on the Haymarket in London. This was a wonderful commission. It also led to my first one-man exhibition in the Redfern Gallery in London's West End.

Rex Nan Kivell was a New Zealander who started the Redfern Gallery between the two world wars. He was also a well-known collector of modern European paintings, as well as of early historic paintings from the Pacific. He was a great encouragement to me, and my exhibition at the Redfern Gallery was a success. At the end of it Nan Kivell said to me that I should have another exhibition in a year's time. This made me feel somewhat frightened! By now I had got to know a lot about the kind of 'type-casting' required for British artists to be recognised and promoted by the critics and the art fraternity. I was scared that the price of possible fame in that society would limit my freedom to paint as I felt. I knew then that perhaps the best way for me to retain artistic freedom would be to return to New Zealand.

I was, however, honoured by the Redfern Gallery by being included in their summer exhibitions, hanging paintings alongside Picasso, Mondrian, Matisse, Max Ernst, Modigliani, Roualt and many other famous artists. It may have been because I had lived in France that I felt strangely more at home with the European artists than I did amongst the British.

It was during the time that I was working on the mural for New Zealand House that my feelings were drawn very closely to New Zealand again. I had been away from it for some years, and this combined with the fact that I could never really become part of another society made me know that New Zealand was my home. My feelings were in conflict with Tanya's understandable attitudes about coming to live in New Zealand. After all, my knowledge of the meaning of 'home' was exactly the same for her. But somehow, because of me, she had to live on the other side of the world from her 'home'. For many years to come it was a difficult choice.

On our return in late 1963 it took me some time to adjust to living again in New Zealand. For Tanya it took much longer. It seemed a strange, empty place to us both. Already back from London were Brian Carmody, Pat Hanly, Don Peebles and Ralph

Hotere. Some, such as Bill Culbert, Michael Brown and Robert MacDonald, never returned to live here and are now almost forgotten in their own home country. Later Jeanne Benseman was to return.

In the years from the mid-fifties to the mid-sixties during which I was away, some important changes had taken place. In Auckland Kees and Tine Hos had opened the New Vision Gallery, Don Woods the Ikon Gallery and Barry Lett the Uptown Gallery. The Centre Gallery was still operating in Wellington, but there were no proper dealer galleries until Elva Bett and Catherine Duncan set up the Bett Duncan Gallery at the same time as Peter McLeavey set up his. Much later Janne Land established her gallery, and Kay Roberts took over the Brooker Gallery where I have continued to exhibit my paintings.

When I came back I started teaching at the School of Design, which was under the leadership of James Coe. Polytechnics were new and their policy was to teach subjects with a direct vocational justification. I didn't fit into this slot in education very well.

I had always believed that teaching and learning should have positive effects on the growth of imagination in an adventurous way. For a long time I felt that my teaching of drawing, painting and printmaking at the Polytechnic was tolerated as a fringe activity. I had always regarded these subjects, together with sculpture, as basic to the students' understanding of art and design. The students were a remarkable bunch of young, talented people, but what could I give them? I kept thinking about Leonardo as an inventor, and of Matisse, not only as a painter and sculptor, but also as the designer of a beautiful chapel. And I kept thinking of Le Corbusier, who thought of himself as a painter more than he thought of himself as an architect. I thought, too, of the restrictions that were imposed on the imagination of our young students to justify the kind of education they were having. Slowly, but noticeably, the leaders in education and art education were becoming faceless and anonymous. It was different from the days of enlightenment I had had under the influences of C.E. Beeby, Gordon Tovey, Doreen Blumhardt and Walter Scott.

When I arrived back, my friends, relatives and colleagues in teaching and painting said, 'Oh, John, you haven't changed at all!' How could I possibly begin to tell them how I had? I could never see things in the way I had before! It was a bit like that, too, with the response to my more abstract paintings and prints. For a long time people couldn't understand them, and I couldn't explain them either.

If we were to continue to live and work in New Zealand we needed a house with separate studio space, hopefully on the flat and yet with a view. We were very fortunate in finding just what we wanted: an old house with plenty of space, in Island Bay, by the sea, looking out onto Cook Strait. This has been a continuing joy and inspiration for Tanya, for me and now for our children. Where else in the world could it be like this? The atmosphere and the change of every day is different.

Painting the mural for New Zealand House in London was a forerunner to other commissions in New Zealand. In 1969 I was asked to produce a large kinetic mural for the entrance to the New Zealand Pavilion at Expo '70 in Osaka, Japan. This work, somewhat re-vamped, is now permanently installed in the entrance foyer of the National Library, in Wellington. Then in 1973 I had the task of producing my biggest, most long-term commission. This was the mural for the banqueting hall and the Members' dining room of the Beehive, or less colloquially the Executive Wing of Parliament. It was a huge job in every way! It took me more than three years to complete, and because I had to teach at the same time I was exhausted at the end of it. It was also a frightening responsibility. A mural is very different from a picture on a wall which you could take down when you were tired of it. However, the challenge to produce such a huge and important public work was exhilarating. It was only in New Zealand that I would have had the opportunity of such an extraordinary experience.

In my other work of printmaking I had for some years been able to organise and teach evening classes at the School of Design. Adult artists would come and join with the full-time younger students to work together. I felt that William Johnson from the Central School in London would have approved of this. Artists such as Kate Coolahan, Janet Paul, Penny Ormerod, Shona McFarlane, John Lethbridge and Susan Skerman shared their ideas, and they all produced some remarkably innovative work.

For many years now New Zealand printmakers have partici-
pated in International Biennales all over the world. In one of these
exhibitions, at Lugano in Switzerland, I won a major prize. Previous prize-winners in this particular exhibition had included Giorgio
Morandi, Ben Nicholson and David Hockney, and I began to feel
again part of the international 'club' of artists, although so far away
from it. It was much easier to show prints than it was to send paintings overseas. Since living in New Zealand I have been able to
participate in exhibitions in Poland, Yugoslavia, Argentina, India,
Japan, the USA and the UK. Other printmakers such as Barry
Cleavin, Stanley Palmer, Kate Coolahan, Marilynn Webb and Gary
Tricker have done the same. Strangely enough, our participation
in these important exhibitions around the world has never been
mentioned in our local press – unlike our sporting exploits.

Even now exhibiting here in New Zealand is like a fresh start
each time. Our critics and commentators do not follow with any
critical continuity the lives and works of our artists. I think that
there is probably a great deal of interesting, important and
innovative work going on in the visual arts in New Zealand, but
who knows?

I feel now that in New Zealand I have been lucky enough to
carry out in my own work some of the things I have always
believed in through my teaching. It has been here that I have not
only been able to paint and to print, but also I have been given
the opportunity to produce murals, stained-glass windows,
sculptured walls and floor rugs. I feel, too, that in living here I
have been able to retain the freedoms, and hopefully avoid the
stereotypes, of being an artist.

In 1963 it could never have occurred to me that one of the reasons for my attention being drawn back to New Zealand would
follow me home from London. In 1991 the interior of New Zealand House was being reconstructed, and the government decided to send my large mural to Wellington. It is now
permanently housed in the National Archives building. I feel
very much at home with this work being here, with me, in New
Zealand. But the question remains with me – would I ever have
come back to New Zealand if I had not painted this mural? It
was instrumental in my return.

# The Baptist Is Back

## Rodney Macann

It started in February 1988. I was in Adelaide to sing at the Festival, in a very unusual opera by Prokofiev, *The Fiery Angel*. My home at this time was England, High Wycombe, in Buckinghamshire. I'd been living in England for twenty-two years.

Opera singers when they are away from home often have quite a bit of spare time; after all, you only sing every two or three days once performances have begun. The strain of singing over a large orchestra, unaided by amplification, normally means that in a large role you need a day or two to recover. I loved Adelaide; the warmth, the open sky, the beaches, the friendliness of the people, the layout of the city. It reminded me a great deal of my home town, Christchurch. In fact they both had the same street plan and the similarities abounded. Essentially I was enjoying being in the Antipodes.

I wrote to some very good friends in Wellington, John and Jenny Boshier, told them of my enjoyment of Adelaide and as a throwaway, semi-flippant remark at the end of the letter said something like, 'I'm enjoying being back down-under so much, if Tom Cadman leaves Central let me know and I'll come and be your minister.' (Tom Cadman was the minister of Wellington Central Baptist Church. John and Jenny were members of that church. I, in addition to being an opera singer, was an ordained Baptist minister, but more of that later.)

Back in High Wycombe, and just prior to Christmas 1988, we had our usual Christmas letter from the Boshiers, with a brief line at the end: 'Guess what, Rod? Tom is leaving Central – are you interested?' Then a couple of days before Christmas John Boshier rang to wish us well for Christmas, or so he said. When I heard his voice, something deep inside told me this was more than just a Christmas call and he duly came to the point – would I allow him to put my name forward for the position of minister at Wellington Central? I remember my response. In a sense I thought I was safe from upheaval. 'I'm not uninterested, but can't envisage things proceeding, as I'm not free to move for eighteen months and no one else at your church knows me.' But I had a strange premonition that we might in fact be moving to Wellington.

Wellington as a city had always appealed to me and if a career move back to ministry was to take place, a central-city church seemed the natural place for me to operate, given my own gifts and experience. But to leave the English National Opera and Covent Garden would be a wrench, and to move back after twenty-two years would take courage.

There had always been a part of me that wanted to return to New Zealand. Every so often that part had asserted itself. There were many trips over the years, initially with a fiancée, then a wife and one daughter, two daughters, two daughters and a son, two daughters, a son and a pregnant wife. On one of those trips I came ahead by myself. It was during a period of dissatisfaction with grey skies and opera singing and I all but bought my general practitioner wife, Lorna, a practice in Auckland, and greeted her with the news when she arrived. However, that was really a pipe dream and was set aside, and over the years I gradually came to terms with the fact that Britain was now my home. I even had my own little bit of 'imitation' New Zealand to keep me from pining too much. In about 1986 I was singing with Scottish Opera. Lorna and the family joined me for a long holiday weekend and we were driving around the wonderful Scottish countryside. I was reflecting on how much it reminded me of New Zealand and made the comment that I would love to own a log cabin near one of the lochs, in the Scottish hills.

About half an hour later we were driving through a little alpine village, Strathyre, and saw a sign 'Log Cabins for Sale' – we had to investigate.

We saw, we loved, we bought. With the craggy hills, continually changing skies, wonderful lochs and river, Strathyre was my home away from home. Gradually I accepted that I might lay down my bones in the United Kingdom, preferably Scotland. We spent family Christmases at Strathyre, sometimes it snowed, and there were magnificent hoar frosts. We were there in the summer and acquired a collection of kayaks. The river was about twenty feet from the cabin and we could kayak upstream to one loch, downstream to another. For us the place had just about everything. It was part of an old stone village, with very friendly local inhabitants, but also in open country with spectacular walks into the hills only minutes away. In short, after twenty years or so, and largely because of Strathyre, I'd settled down in Britain.

During 1988, after my fateful flippant letter to Wellington, we'd gone to Strathyre for a family holiday and Lorna and I spent some time looking at where we were and where we could see ourselves heading. Life was very good for us. We had our young family, Rachel (9), Katharine (8), Stuart (4) and Robert (2), and we both had fulfilling careers. Lorna was a partner in a thriving medical practice in High Wycombe. I had a contract as principal bass-baritone with the English National Opera, and made frequent guest appearances at Covent Garden and venues outside the United Kingdom. In High Wycombe much of our life revolved around the Baptist Church, and we had a number of good friends in the church, medicine and music. We had a lovely home with about half an acre of ground in the centre of High Wycombe, which itself is set in the beech woods of Buckinghamshire and situated about thirty miles from London and Oxford. We felt settled and yet our own particular philosophy of life dictated that we should never settle down too much, that we should be prepared to move if it seemed right.

We talked about this. Were we too settled? Should I be open to the possibility of moving back into the ministry in the church? In the terms that we spoke and thought, 'What did God want us to do?' I felt that Lorna's work as a general practitioner was very important and we had to have a good reason for leaving Wycombe. Lorna, although very committed to the practice, was prepared to move. She would love to spend more time with the children, she said. No decisions were taken and no plans made, but we quietly resolved that we were willing to move – though we still assumed that it would be somewhere in the United Kingdom.

Then came the Boshier letter and phone call, and a couple of months later someone acting on behalf of Wellington Central Baptist Church contacted me. It was agreed that in June 1989, when I was going to be in New Zealand, I would meet with the deacons of the church to explore possibilities. I duly arrived and stayed a few days with good friends in Auckland. It was unusually cold. I went up to Kerikeri for a couple of days to see my brother, and there was even a frost (and no central heating!). I'd become soft. Did I really want to come back to New Zealand? By that stage I'd lived as long in the United Kingdom as New Zealand, and for most of my adult working life. New Zealand had always seemed so appealing from afar, but now the advantages of living on the doorstep of one of the world's great cities and the close proximity of Europe pressed their claim.

Could I really curtail my singing career? I'd always wanted to move from singing relatively early, rather than see my career wind painfully down, but I was only forty-six.

My career had been somewhat patchy, with great opportunities and promise in the late sixties and early seventies when I'd made major British, American and European concert debuts in the Albert Hall, Carnegie Hall and Berlin Philharmonic. Then I'd stepped back and gone off to Spurgeon's College in 1971 to study theology and prepare for some sort of ministry in the church. There followed eight years as part-time minister at the Baptist Church in High Wycombe, with my singing straggling along with occasional high spots – they were happy, fulfilling years, working with good people – but by 1982 I had completed my work at that church, although we continued a happy but non-professional association. My singing moved steadily on, and by 1989 I was well established in opera, with the United Kingdom as my base. In 1990 I was going to sing in Japan with José Carreras, and at the Bolshoi in Moscow; do several performances in Germany; go to New Zealand for the Festival of the Arts, and back to Covent Garden and the English National Opera.

When I was about fourteen my voice had descended from a low, unmelodic sort of boy soprano to bass-baritone and I started to enjoy singing. One of the songs I loved to sing, because it told of a new-found faith, was 'I'd rather have Jesus than silver or gold . . . I'd rather have Jesus than men's applause . . . I'd rather have Jesus than world-wide fame [there wasn't much chance of that] . . . houses or lands'. It had always seemed to me that I went through life working out the implications of that song. What did it mean now? I was grateful for a faith that in many ways sustained me. I'd been brought up in a Christian home and a very musical one. Christianity and music for me were inseparable. My father was a fine singer and conductor of the Oxford Terrace Baptist Choir. My mother had plenty of drive and gave my two younger brothers and me encouragement to develop and seize opportunities.

When I was thirteen I came to personal faith. It came as a bit of a shock for me to discover that Christianity isn't just something you inherit from your parents or even a church, but is activated by a personal response to Jesus Christ and a commitment to follow Him. Our minister at the Oxford Terrace church in those days was Roland Hart and he was very strongly of the view that God has plans for our lives and that we fulfil our true potential when we are responsive to His will. Our route map through life, he taught, is put together by reading the Bible, prayer, discussion, good sense and proceeding in what seems to be the right direction. Implicit in all of this was the understanding that we should be prepared to change tack if we are convinced it's the right decision. Our route is not fixed.

Was I prepared to change tack and would it be the right decision?

I left my friends in Auckland and flew to Wellington, where I was met by my brother, Stuart, and his wife, Ann. I went out to stay with them and was introduced to a relatively new niece, Emma, who was very apprehensive about this strange guy with a beard. It was late June and cold, and it felt bleak. Wellington looked small and a hotch-potch of a city, little buildings perched precariously on hills and not much evidence of town planning.

The following morning, Sunday, I was collected by a church member and driven in to attend a service at Central. Only the deacons knew officially I was there to meet with them. It was a dismal morning, low cloud or thick fog, and when we arrived the church seemed tiny, like a limpet attached to Press House. I was greeted by Maxwell Collins, whom I'd been in correspondence with, and taken inside to sit with John and Jenny Boshier, still the only folk I knew in the congregation. I was still getting used to all these Kiwi accents and felt slightly disoriented. The service was conducted by Mark Pierson, later to become my associate, and it was good. I could relate to it and liked what he was saying: very direct, compared with British flannel. (I was later to learn that Kiwis generally are direct people. When you leave the country at twenty-three, you haven't learned much about your own kith and kin.) The congregation was smaller than I was expecting and the building unprepossessing by British or even Christchurch standards. However, I had been told it was due to be demolished and the church was moving into a fabulous new complex next door, so I didn't take too much notice. I was taken to meet Mark Pierson, and his wife, Robyn, after the service; he knew why I was there and apparently because of his influence in some areas of the church it was important to gain his seal of approval. We later became good colleagues, although I felt for him with me coming in as leader of the ministry team.

Mid-afternoon I was to meet with the deacons. Being with them was an enjoyable and satisfying experience. I tried to be as frank as possible and we dealt with a number of pertinent issues. I came away from that meeting fairly convinced that a move to Wellington was looming. That evening Maxwell and Barbara Collins invited me back to their apartment perched up in Kelburn, a beautiful spot, with a typically Wellington harbour view. It was the night of the Mobil Song Quest finals and we watched on television. For me that was a very strange experience. Both the competition itself and the friendships forged with other singers such as Kiri Te Kanawa, Malvina Major, Grant Dickson, Patricia Payne and one of my closest friends, Anson Austin, had been important in shaping me as a singer. But that had been twenty-four years before. Watching was agony. I was reliving the nervous anticipation of singing, the long wait for the results, and I feared the American judge, Joan Dorneman, would get it wrong. Somehow watching terrified me. The Mobil Song Quest was a confrontation with my past, and reinforced that I was on my way back. I must have been very dull company, and didn't say much.

The following evening Maxwell very kindly rang me to say that the deacons were going to recommend to the all-important church meeting that they ask me to come as their minister. He intimated that they had come to the decision quite quickly, but subsequently spent some time discussing the fact that they would still want me to have some freedom to pursue my singing career. I rang Lorna and told her the news. The following day I moved down to Christchurch to spend time with my father and to start preparing for ministry in New Zealand. It was still over a year before I would be free to take up the job.

I left the Antipodean winter and flew back to an English summer. The day after I arrived back we drove to the south of France. Lorna and I talked endlessly once we were there, but were careful not yet to say anything in front of the children. It looked certain that I would be invited to become minister of Wellington Central Baptist Church. What would our response be? Lorna, without having seen the situation, was keen, for although she was English she loved New Zealand and had always warmed to the prospect of living there. After my initial apprehension about moving back, I too was becoming more enthusiastic. It was a good time to move back: a year before Rachel was due to start secondary school and about the same before Robert started primary school. And if I was to make a career shift, it had to be now, while I was young enough to give it energy and enthusiasm. Then there was the church itself. I had no reservations. A church is people and I had responded positively to the people and felt at one with them. It was also a challenging situation with loads of potential: Central's was an extraordinarily able congregation which, I believed, played an important part in the life of the city. An old maxim for decision-making came to the fore: write down the pros and cons. We didn't really come up with any cons. After all, there was the huge bonus of living back in Godzone, and in Wellington, a small but beautiful and vibrant city, centre of the arts in New Zealand and with the sort of climate that would never allow boredom or torpor.

When we got back to High Wycombe there was a letter waiting from the church. They did want me to come. I said to Lorna, 'Well?', and she said matter-of-factly, 'We've already decided, haven't we?' And we had.


Music in New Zealand has always been very strong at the grass roots, and our choirs have been an expression of the commitment of many Kiwis to music-making. In the mid-1960s the large choral societies abounded. Christchurch, my home city, had two very fine choirs, and in 1965 New Zealand was asked to send a choir to the great Commonwealth Arts Festival in Britain. The Christchurch Harmonic Society was chosen, and I was invited to join them. While we were in London I was offered a singing contract by the BBC. I came back to Christchurch, gave in my notice at the Bank of New Zealand, and early in 1966 embarked on a new career in a new country. It was exciting. Malvina Major, Kiri Te Kanawa, Patricia Payne, Anson Austin and I all went to Britain around the same time and in different ways spurred each other on. I effectively served my musical apprenticeship with the BBC Singers, resigning in 1969 as my concert career in Britain and Europe developed.

This was a wonderful period of my life, but also a very unsettling one. My career was developing, Lorna and I had become engaged, and my working holiday visa, already over-extended, ran out and I had to return home in 1970 for a few months, during which time I made my opera debut with the New Zealand Opera Company in *The Barber of Seville*, with Malvina Major. I returned to England in May 1970 and Lorna and I were duly married on 1 August at Dagnall Street Baptist Church, St Albans in Hertfordshire – a glorious English summer's day, from many points of view.

We then moved to Edinburgh where Lorna was studying medicine. Very few of us, it seems, make major changes in our lives without strong incentives or external factors. When I became a singer, a door was effectively opened and I walked through; when I fell in love with Lorna the most natural chase was joined. Coming to Wellington would be because I was invited. But in 1971 restlessness set in. I steadily became convinced that I should set aside a full-time singing career and study for the church. I did not fully or even partly understand what was happening to me. I had had a strong interest in ministry before, but never the conviction that I should train, and it seemed strange timing on the part of the Almighty if I was to try to follow His way. I was on the threshold of a major singing career, the preparatory work had been done. The minister of Lorna's home church in St Albans, a dry old cynic, Dr Morris West, suggested I might just be running away from earning money and visible success. I didn't see it that way. We only have one life, in this world anyway, and increasingly I wanted to do more than sing, wonderful though that is.

Lorna and I had been open about possible career shifts when we married. We had talked about the church and now she supported me. So I went down to Spurgeon's College in London to study theology for three years and Lorna transferred to St Mary's, Paddington, to continue her study. We were students together. Over the next few years I frequently wondered what on earth I was doing at Spurgeon's. The principal, George Beasley-Murray, was an enthusiastic musician and encouraged me to continue with my singing career as much as possible. So I would return from a concert, the applause, the egocentric buzz that singing gave, and be hauled over the coals for my bad Greek. Spurgeon's was stultifyingly conservative. I'd gone there primarily because of Beasley-Murray, whom I greatly admired, and because it was in London and I could still keep in touch with singing. Stuck out on Norwood Hill, at times it seemed miles removed from the real world, and some of my young fellow students were so rigid they had the demeanour of fossils. Some of the lecturers, by contrast, were creative and stimulating and I pitied them having to deal with an ignoramus like myself and bigots like some of the others. Three years passed, at times very slowly. What to do at the end of it? The High Wycombe Baptist Church took the major decision-making out of my hands and asked me to join them as associate, part-time minister, responsible for a large youth group and various other tasks. Lorna and I could see no reason for not going to High Wycombe and we never had any regrets. Eight remarkably fulfilling and happy years passed quickly as minister/ singer.


We decided to delay telling the family of our decision to go to Wellington as long as possible, not wanting to unsettle them. However, I felt committed to letting my agent and the English National Opera know fairly soon, as both had plans for me several years ahead. Lorna also felt that her partner at the practice in High Wycombe had to be given good notice. We decided on October. My agent and Peter Jonas, the managing director of the English National, were amazingly understanding and even seemed to share in my growing excitement about the move back to New Zealand. I began to wonder if I hadn't been singing as well as I might have thought. The reaction of my colleagues generally was also interested and supportive. Many of them understood that, wonderfully fulfilling though the music profession is, there are other aspects of us that want expression too. One gripe that I had with being a singer was that in a sense, no matter how successful you were, you were never allowed to grow up. You always have a conductor or producer telling you what to do, imposing their will on you, although of course the best directors (even some Germans) would treat the work as a partnership, exploring together a new role. Another hang-up was the wasted time. It is impossible to plan a truly accurate rehearsal schedule for opera, and the endless hours that were spent in canteens expecting to be called at any moment as your scene approached were a source of frustration.

Opera is, too, in many ways an élitist art form and the fact that I was often performing to a very small, affluent group of people, particularly in a house like Covent Garden, at times disturbed me. Many of my singing colleagues understood these things very well, and while I had thought they might see me as going off at an inexplicable tangent, they did not. Their reaction was heart-warming and in its own way an affirmation of our decision.

Word of it was now spreading and we still hadn't told the children. We certainly did not want them to hear second-hand. We decided to take our daughters out for a meal. I forget why it worked out this way, but we had a meal in London before a performance of *The Magic Flute*, and after the performance they came with me to Heathrow where I caught a flight to Dusseldorf for a *Fidelio* performance. The girls' reaction was interesting. They simply did not believe us. They thought we were kidding. After an hour or so of discussion they started to believe us, but accepting the decision took a great deal longer. We were back in Wellington for at least a year before we felt our daughters were showing signs of being settled. Stuart, our five-year-old son, wondered if he would have to learn a new language. He and Robert in fact learned very quickly. During the 1991 Rugby World Cup, I asked them who they would support, these two young Englishmen. 'The All Blacks, of course,' came the answer. Such is peer pressure.

As we served out our last year, there was at times a degree of escapism. The traffic wouldn't be like this in Wellington; Lorna was looking forward to more time with the family; I was looking forward to the time when I could be a normal human being. As a singer so much of your focus has to be on your own performance, there is inevitable anxiety about the state of your voice. On performance days you tend to shut out the rest of the world as you prepare for those two hours of high concentration on stage. If you're singing a major role, it takes hours to wind down afterwards. You are vulnerable, sensitive to what others will think of your performance, audience reaction and at times critics' reaction – you want to please, stimulate, communicate, challenge, establish bonds with your audience. Inevitably, you're so locked into what you're doing that relationships suffer and at times those close to you need to be understanding. I was becoming increasingly impatient with this aspect of the life – I wanted to enjoy a cold, shout myself hoarse, not wander round in my own little world. C'mon Wellington! Did I really think being a minister was so normal and so free? I should have remembered my last year as minister at High Wycombe. The family really had owned very little of me then . . .

The year between acceptance and departure seemed to drag; our thoughts were already in Wellington. Lorna and I came out for two weeks in March 1990 because I was singing in the International Festival of the Arts. We looked at houses, met with church folk and again confirmed how much we were looking forward to our move in August.

The last few months had highlights. For me there was singing my final performance with the English National Opera at the Bolshoi in Moscow, in one of my favourite operas, *Xerxes*. There was a touching moment when Mark Elder, our charismatic and gifted music director, had a chat and told me how special I was to him because when he had first heard me he never thought I would make an opera singer. Then in July 'New Zealand at Covent Garden' was shown on television in New Zealand and prepared the way for my return in an interesting way. Kiri Te Kanawa, interviewed before the programme, said how good it was to be with old friends, and how she and Rodney had reminisced about how close they came to marrying each other and what a disaster it would have been!

My ministry commenced at Wellington Central Baptist Church on Sunday, 19 August 1990. I walked into the church to lead the worship and preach. We were members of a new family, a family of many different nationalities, a family that explores the future together, that seeks to understand its role and minister to the city.

At the time of writing we have been back about twenty months. People often ask if I have any regrets. I have none. I realise that there was much that I didn't know about my country when I returned. Coming back to New Zealand just prior to the 1990 general election quickly reinforced that, but I am learning. I am learning to live again in one of the most genuinely egalitarian societies in the world, where we cut down tall poppies, where every year I lose a number of younger members of my congregation as they too leave to get their Overseas Experience, where there has been and is a developing consciousness of what it means to be a New Zealander. I have had many barbecues, eaten more ice cream, taken up regular squash again, and gloried in the Wellington harbour and bush. I am not only a Kiwi but a Wellingtonian.

I have continued to sing (I hope not too much) back at Covent Garden, with the Australian opera companies and orchestras and, perhaps most satisfying of all, at the 1992 Wellington International Festival of the Arts: the role of 'John the Baptist' in the Richard Strauss opera, *Salome*. A publicity gimmick? No – the Baptist is no longer 'crying in the wilderness': the Baptist is safely back home.

# To Have Both Hemispheres

## Malvina Major

I have sung all my life. All my family sang. I was born the seventh of eight children, and my mother and father were both intensely musical. In fact had they been born a little later and had they had greater opportunities, they might have had musical careers. As it was, music was the centre of our family life, and my mother harboured the secret ambition that at least one of her children might be properly trained and have a professional life in music.

Because I came towards the end of the family, all that went before me is hearsay. I know, however, that the first six children were born in Christchurch or Dunedin, and because of the Depression the family went to the West Coast where Dad got a job as head cowman and Mum as head cook at a sanatorium. When the Second World War came, the family moved north and Dad and my eldest brother, John, got work in the ammunition factory at Hamilton, where I was born. My eldest sister had married by that time so remained in the South Island, and her first child, my nephew, was born just four months later than I was. My brother, Daryl, five years younger than I, had nieces and nephews older than himself.

Our eldest brother, John, specialised in George Formby songs, and when he was young in Dunedin he used to entertain the people across the road in the pub from his bedroom window. When he got to Hamilton he and Eric Struckett, who played the violin, worked up a comic musical act called 'The Major and the Minor' which they toured through hospitals, pubs, prisons and in talent quests. Then Betty, Donald and I formed a trio. Betty was about ten years my senior and Donald about five years. Betty taught us both to play the ukelele and the guitar, and how to yodel. We first sang and performed as a group on the newly opened radio station in Hamilton, when I was two. That was less memorable an event, perhaps, than my first stage appearance in the Hamilton State Theatre. My mother thought I was too young, but my father agreed to my request to join in. (I think he wasn't really paying attention to what I was saying, and in any case he always said 'yes' to whatever I asked for. Of all eight children I was probably the one who got closest to him.) I ruined the item really because my pants kept falling down and I kept hitching them up: the audience broke up.

Despite this inauspicious start, Betty and Donald let me stay in the trio and we entertained all who would listen – returned servicemen, old people's homes, hospitals, church groups, wedding receptions, conferences. Stage work for me was just a part of life, like going to school. Even in our home, when people came to visit or stay my mother would say, 'You must entertain them', and we did.

There were two pianos in our house, one of which belonged to Dick Hunt, a man who played a big part in our lives. He was a railway worker at Frankton Junction who came to live with us when I was about a year old and stayed on when we had grown up. He even lived with my father after my mother died. His fiancée had been killed while horse riding a fortnight before he was due to marry, and I think he never got over it. Certainly he never married, and we became a surrogate family for him while he generously enhanced all our lives. He was a marvellous piano player himself, and though he taught me a little he thought I should be taught 'properly' so paid for my first formal lessons. He also taught us all to ride bikes, and bought one for each of us, for which he built sidecars or trailers to carry our gear. My piano teacher, Mrs Bateman, had a piano accordion band she wanted me to join, so Dick bought me my first beautiful blue accordion, which I still have. My playing with Mrs Bateman's band in dance halls and for Scottish dancing clubs did not overly impress my mother, who thought I should stick to the piano. However, my brothers thought it was wonderful, and Dick on piano, Darryl on drums, and I formed another band and played all over the Waikato. Music was our life.

We were a very close family and music was the cement that bound us. Although we were Presbyterians my mother was convinced that the nuns were the best music teachers. When I was in standard three or four we moved from Hamilton to a small farm at Te Kowhai. From there I attended the nearest convent, which was at Ngaruawahia, and learned the piano from Sister Magdalen. During the course of preparation for a formal Royal College exam I had to do ear tests, and suddenly Sister Magdalen realised I could sing. She cross-examined me and was astonished to learn that I sang and yodelled and played the ukelele in public at least two or three times each week. She taught me my first classical song, 'Have You Seen but a White Lily Grow?', entered me in the Hamilton competitions, and I won. Alas, she shortly thereafter contracted tuberculosis so didn't teach me for very long.

Throughout my secondary school years I had two music teachers, Sister Liguori for piano, and Mother Febronie for singing. They were busy years because I sat annual piano, theory and singing exams, as well as academic exams at school, of course, and I continued entertaining often too. At about this stage the Music Society of Hamilton began badgering my mother to send me to Auckland for further training with Sister (later Dame) Mary Leo. I was most reluctant to leave my dear nuns who had been so kind to me and with whom I had got on so well. In fact I had come to love the life of the convent and its atmosphere, but I think Mother Febronie in her heart of hearts felt she had done all she could for me. It was a difficult break for us both.

So at sixteen I auditioned for the famous Sister Mary Leo. My terror was lessened somewhat by the knowledge that she had already heard me sing in the Thames competitions, and presumably would not have agreed to the audition if she thought I was hopeless. She agreed on the spot to take me, and reassured my anxious mother that no, she would not alter my voice. I remember this odd question and answer vividly, for what is teaching and training the voice if it is not altering and improving it and maximising its potential?

And so began a quite arduous period in my life. I went to school four days a week, but travelled to Auckland each Friday for hours with the kind but austere and somewhat daunting Sister Leo. I was so timorous that I think it took about a year before I was able to relax sufficiently really to listen to what she wanted me to do. She was very strict, and lessons with her were very hard work. She always had another nun or student present as accompanist and we just worked and worked on voice production and breathing. She had forbidden me to sing in public for at least twelve months and I found that quite a deprivation, but understood her reasons. She had also forbidden me to sing any of the old songs I knew as she feared that might mean going back to old habits. So I learned a whole new repertoire and a new technique of voice production. It took some time but gradually it clicked into place and I began singing the way she wanted me to. I could really hear the difference. I realised I was singing better than I had before, and also that my range had expanded and I could sing a lot of high notes I had not formerly been able to reach. Sister taught me to throw the sound outside the mask of the face, and to listen to my voice outside my head. It was quite different and I began to hear myself perhaps as others heard me. She also concentrated on breathing techniques and diction, and I began the formidable business of learning Italian and German, both languages I would need if I were to sing opera. I still work on them, even though I now speak them quite well, and I have also had to grapple with French.

In my second, third and fourth years with Sister Leo she allowed me to sing in public and to enter competitions. I reached the zenith of competition singing in New Zealand in 1963 by winning the Mobil Song Quest. Sister said, 'Well, now you must move on. You must go to Australia', and she meant it. I was in a bit of a panic state at the prospect. I had never left home, or my mother, and in addition I met Winston, my future husband, at about that time. Perhaps through fear of change I asked Sister if I might become a nun because I so loved the peace and tranquillity of the convent. She very wisely suggested I should wait until I was twenty-one. In the event I was then married and embarked on an international singing career.

In 1964 I set off to compete in the Sydney and Melbourne Sun Aria competitions. I came second in the Sydney contest by one mark and was dispirited, homesick and pining for my family and Winston. Sister Leo realised I was not in a good state of mind so asked unprecedented permission from her Order to travel alone to help me. My initial delight at seeing her soon waned, however, because she began badgering, criticising and goading me in ways she had never done before. I could not believe it, and grew very angry. Everything I did she seemed to pull to pieces, and I was in tears more often than not. On the night of the competition I ignored her, I was so cross and hurt. I decided I would sing for everyone else, but not for her, and that I would never ever go to lessons with her again.

Well, as I walked off the stage of the Melbourne Town Hall after they had announced that I had won, she was in the wings and threw her arms around me. She would not let me go and cried with joy. She said, 'I know I've been simply awful and bullying to you, but it was exactly what you needed. I knew you were so homesick and miserable that if I sympathised with you, you would simply have wallowed in your own self-pity and not done justice to your talents or training. I had to goad you into sufficient anger and competitiveness not to let yourself down.' Much as I hated to admit it, she was right.

The Sun Aria contest was a launching pad for singers. The prize was £1200 towards tuition costs (the Mobil Song Quest prize had been £300 cash). Sister Leo was a great friend of James Robertson, sometime conductor of the New Zealand Symphony Orchestra, and subsequently founder of the London Opera Centre. She wrote to ask his advice about where I should go and he replied, 'Send her here. There are good teachers in London and I shall take care of her.' And he did.

In the meantime I returned home and married Winston. He then worked with the New Zealand Dairy Company and planned to go to Massey University to study. When I won the Sun Aria contest, however, he immediately put his own ambitions on hold and said he would come to London with me. He was not at all musical himself, but he felt all talents were God-given and should be encouraged. He was quite remarkably generous in that he didn't at all count the cost of that to his own aspirations, but was prepared to do any job just to keep us going.

On James Robertson's advice I studied with Professor Ruth Packer. One of the stresses on me at that time was the question of whether I was a lyric soprano or a mezzo. Sister Leo had felt strongly that I was a lyric soprano and James Robertson concurred, but various other people debated the point, as I had a very strong lower register too. I had two voices, really. In 1966 I won the Kathleen Ferrier Scholarship (she was a mezzo) and the prize money helped pay for a few more months' tuition, which was very expensive.

I got my big break into the international opera circuit by singing the part of Matilda in Rossini's *Elizabetta Regina d'Inghilterra* in the Camden Festival. I was heard there by people who were casting for the Salzburg Festival and was offered the part of Rosina in *The Barber of Seville*. Claudio Abbado from the La Scala Opera House was the conductor and he urged me to go back to Italy with him for further mezzo parts. It was very tempting – La Scala is one of the temples of opera – but James Robertson was adamantly discouraging, saying it would ruin my voice. He was also dismissive of another tempting offer I had at that time, to tour America with the D'Oyly Carte Company, doing seven different soprano leads. I thought it would be a wonderful acting opportunity, and in some ways my entire life might have been different had I taken it. However, James Robertson again said I mustn't. In his view if I went into Gilbert and Sullivan, 'authentic' opera companies would never take me seriously. This crazy distinction between light opera and grand opera has now worn down – some opera stars even record pop songs – but then the conventions were more strict. A third frustration came when I was offered the part of Donna Anna in *Don Giovanni* at Glyndebourne. James Robertson vetoed that, too, on the grounds that the part was too big and I would force my voice.

My spirits picked up with a return to Salzburg for the 1969 Festival, and before my departure Covent Garden made me an offer to do Rosina in *The Barber of Seville* again. However, in my absence the business of whether I was a lyric or mezzo soprano was again debated. I shall never know what really happened, but the offer was withdrawn. I was devastated. To sing at Covent Garden had been my highest adolescent aspiration. I had got so close, only to be deeply disappointed. I felt really let down by Covent Garden and, though other offers and opportunities immediately presented themselves, Winston and I both felt like coming home. We had been based in London for four and a half years, we both wanted to have the sort of strong family life we had enjoyed as children, and I was promised plenty of work in New Zealand with the orchestra, with broadcasting and with the opera company (which was shortly to fold). Additionally, and most importantly, Winston could have his longed-for farm. I felt he had sacrificed his interests long enough for mine and it was about time we jointly pursued his goals. Once the decision was made, it felt right.

My son Andrew was five when Alethea was born, and fifteen months later I had Lorraine. Our family was complete. With two babies and the New Zealand Opera Company defunct, I felt rather trapped, but the symphony orchestra and Broadcasting Corporation honoured their promises to give me plenty of work, and I did a lot of oratorio work too. In the day-to-day life of the farm I was also directly involved. Visiting overseas conductors and soloists sometimes remarked that I didn't look as if I helped muck out cowsheds, and I replied that not only did I wear rubber boots but rubber gloves as well.

I realised that in order to keep my voice at any sort of international or even national level, I would have to do more performing on a regular basis. I went round all the schools in the district and asked whether they would like me to take the children for music. I trained hundreds of children, took them to festivals, mounted concerts and pantomimes with them, and ran a television programme called 'The Malvina Show'. My own children were involved in all this activity, and over the years I raised thousands and thousands of dollars for Lions and Rotary

73

Clubs to spend on good works and charities. I now see that I was burning the candle at both ends. I was doing the odd opera and oratorio, touring the country, training school children and looking after my own, milking the cows with Winston and helping on the farm. All of a sudden I found that my health had gone to pieces. I went down badly and felt I had reached the end of the road. For eighteen months I was a shadow of my usual self and had to turn down all invitations and outside obligations.

Winston, however, was determined that I should recover and simply never accepted that my career was over. When I began to pick up strength a little he took me on holiday to Sydney and made me tour the Opera House. 'Wouldn't you like to sing here?' he urged. At that stage I said I never wanted to sing anywhere again, nor even lift the lid of a piano.

Gradually, though, I got back some confidence and strength. I toured the country with the symphony orchestra in Verdi's *Requiem*, the other splendid soloists being Heather Begg, Donald McIntyre and Anthony Benfell. Inquiries came in from overseas – from San Francisco, London, Paris. Not yet fully fit, I set off on an audition tour but really only got as far as Paris. I had lost a lot of weight, could hardly stand up and was auditioning in the Paris Opera! Unbeknown to me, people from the Brussels Opera House were present and they came backstage to offer me the soprano role in *La Finta Giardiniera*. I've done it fifty or sixty times with them since, along with several other roles, and it has been a long and very happy association. Brussels led to other European opera houses, to a return to Salzburg, to tours of the United States and to Australia. When I started working internationally again, Winston got help on the farm so that he could be with me at least some of the time. Everyone in Brussels and Salzburg met him and thought he was great. When he died suddenly they were all on the phone saying, 'Don't give up your singing. We are looking forward to your coming this summer. You have lots of friends here, and we shall look after you.' They have all been wonderful, terribly supportive, and I feel they have been just like part of my family.

When I think about it, I am absolutely certain Winston had some sort of premonition of his sudden and premature death.

He was so convinced that I would get back to my singing, so determined that I would have a life of my own, so encouraging for me to renew my international work and contacts. My three older sisters all lost their husbands, and on each occasion he got very agitated and started giving advice. 'If anything happens to me, don't stay on the farm. Buy a house in town and immerse yourself in your music.' I would calm him with 'We are so much younger than they are. You are only forty-something. We still have a lifetime together', but he was not reassured.

We went to my niece's wedding on Saturday, 8 September 1990, and had a marvellous time. I sang 'Ave Maria' in the church and with tears in his eyes he said, 'I've never heard you sound better.' At the reception we danced until the early hours of the morning, as we used to do when we were young. On the way home in the car he did not feel well, but on Sunday was fine. At 9 a.m. on Monday he was gone. I just couldn't believe it. In fact it took more than a year for it to really hit me, and for me to grieve properly and begin to come to terms with the reality. My children, who are twenty, twenty-one and twenty-six, have been absolutely wonderful, but of course it is a great loss for them too. My son is finishing some building work he is involved in, but plans to come back to run the farm. My elder daughter has recently married and will run my home in New Plymouth when I am travelling. My younger daughter couldn't bear the sudden absence of her father so has gone to explore Australia.

In many ways I am at a turning point in my life, and it has been an horrific time. My daughter-in-law lost her baby (it was our first grandchild), then Winston died three weeks later. Just a few months after that both my sisters died within a fortnight of each other. How does one cope with such grief and shock? Singing is supposed to be joyous. How does one ever sing again?

I have thought a lot about why I came back to New Zealand, why I am based here, and why I am now back on the international opera circuit. Everyone needs to feel truly based in place and family, especially expressive artists who must draw continuously on their inner resources. It was right for me to give our children a proper family life, and for Winston to pursue his love of farming. It was possible for me, even if difficult, to continue to sing and to preserve my voice. Modern transport makes it possible now for me to keep my New Zealand base and to perform anywhere. I'm not much further from Brussels in terms of time and cost than if I lived in, say, Helsinki. I live in the most isolated and beautiful country on earth, but it is only a plane ride from anywhere.

Sister Mary Leo was fully supportive when I first came back and said to her, 'I've given away my international career.' She pointed out that I had a good husband and could continue to sing here. She didn't reproach me at all, or make it any more difficult for me. However, when I went to see her to tell her I was going back overseas to sing (and she was old and unwell by that stage) she was just ecstatic. She was so excited and said she wanted to see Winston to tell him face-to-face what a great person she thought he was. She knew that trying to go back after fifteen years' absence would be difficult, but she had faith in me and never doubted I would succeed.

My aim now is to gain as much knowledge as I can so that I may pass it on; to take care of my voice so that it may last as long as possible, to seize opportunities that present themselves, and to treasure each musical moment. One of my immediately exciting prospects is to work with Richard Bonynge in *Lucia di Lammermoor*, and if that goes well we are talking about *Norma* and *La Somnambula*. I feel the music of Bellini and Donazetti really suits my voice, so perhaps a new chapter of my life is just opening. I have just sung Donna Anna in Christchurch under the watchful eye of the very talented Canadian conductor, Brian Law. For the first time in two years I feel I have regained my total voice and love of life and singing. My *Lucia* will benefit from this regained strength. Salzburg have also invited me back for the Festival, and I have recitals planned in London and Vienna, and at Expo in Seville. The schedule is very full and busy.

When I come back to New Zealand in the northern autumn I am going to launch the Malvina Major Foundation to help train singers and musicians and people in all the other skills necessary to mount opera. I shall start fundraising again – I've done a lot of it in my time – and we hope to endow scholarships to train people with talent either here or overseas.

When I have toured in tiny towns in New Zealand, quite often people discover opera isn't something to be in awe of; it is something they can enjoy. The fact too that I have kept my New Zealand address is noted by opera singers and opera companies on the other side of the world. They think, 'Well, if she can stay there, and thrive there, it can't be the cultural desert we imagined.' More and more successful New Zealanders have found that they can both live here and enjoy an international singing career. Others have told me that they too are thinking of coming home. That has to be good for all of us. Musical life in general, and opera in particular, is flourishing in both Australia and New Zealand and I'm sure we have a fine future. New generations of singers will not feel the terrible need for choice between the southern and northern hemispheres that I did. They will be able to have both.

One last thing I should perhaps stress is that I'm not a snob, and I don't want to be confined to the exclusive box labelled 'grand opera'. I like all kinds of music: good ballads, oratorio, Lieder and recital work. I think *entertaining* is the thing I like most; getting a good rapport with my audience. It goes right back to my early childhood training at home, to my mother saying, 'You must entertain them, Malvina.'

# To See Clearly

## Robin Morrison

---

Had I the heaven's embroidered cloths
Enwrought with gold and silver light,
The blue and the dim and the dark cloths
of night and light and the half light.

*W.B. Yeats*

Your relationship with your place of birth is always complex and probably changes with time and with the perspective distance gives. Similarly your relationship with the place forebears came from – in my case Ireland – is also complex. Since my teenage years I have been fascinated by the writings of the poets and novelists of the Irish renaissance; in particular by the poems of W.B. Yeats and the novels of James Joyce. To be able to write intensely about Dublin, Joyce had first to go into exile, as it were, in Paris. To be able to see New Zealand, really see it, I had first to go into a kind of exile too, and interestingly enough our literary renaissance – especially Keri Hulme's *the bone people* – played an important part in my once wanting to come home.

I was Auckland-born and spent much of my childhood there, but my teenage years were spent in Palmerston North. My father was a photographer, but not my sort of photographer. He would never have dreamed of packing a camera and hitting the road to capture a book of photographs as I like to do. He was a home portrait photographer who worked with lights and so on.

He did, however, have a very effective way with people, especially children, and was able to elicit the right responses for very striking portraits.

After a year at Massey University I decided that if I was to grow up I needed to leave home, so I looked around for a subject offered by Otago but not by Massey, and decided on anthropology. That largely accidental choice was hugely important, for it fostered my fascination with the variety of the human condition and taught me that observation could be both a science and an art. Like all of my generation I was keen to explore the big wide world, but I was luckier than most in that I did not even have to save up for my fare. A great aunt died, and the whole family had enough money to set out on the *Ruahine* for a year in Britain.

It was the classic way to travel: not only did it impress on you the vastness of the Pacific and the distance our forebears had travelled from their places of birth to settle in New Zealand, but it gave you a first taste of the exotic tropics before you arrived to London's grey skies and snow. Just dropping into Tahiti made an indelible impression of moist heat, beautiful women, dark skins, the excitement of a foreign language, and also dirt and languor alien to the Dunedin I had come from. We also called into Jamaica on New Year's Eve and the people, drunk on rum, were dancing in the streets and not at all like Dunedin's Presbyterians in their demeanour.

Arriving in London from its former farthest colony in the mid-sixties was very exciting. I didn't mind the cold (indeed I felt it was invigorating), and I could see that Britain was at last climbing out of its post-war depression of the spirit and a whole new generation of young talent was making London the focus for fashion, music, theatre and the arts. The place was bouncing and lively and not at all staid.

I was young and unencumbered and lived a wondrously free existence. Work was easy to pick up, friends were easy to make, and as a New Zealander I had few inhibitions about turning my hand to whatever turned up. I had all sorts of adventures. For instance, once while working on a fishing trawler off the coast of Cornwall I unwittingly got involved in the age-old game of smuggling. A Dutch cargo boat drew astern and my fellow crew pitched in with a will to swap fish for brandy and cigarettes. I wasn't particularly judgemental about what was evidently a well-established procedure, but I did manage to injure my wrist rather badly in the manoeuvres. Another memorable escapade was hitch-hiking to Dublin with a friend in order to visit the haunts of James Joyce. We drank Guinness, slept on park benches and talked endlessly to the locals. Dublin is the most beautiful of cities – it has been preserved because it escaped wartime bombing and the depredations of economic development. Not only is it one of Europe's great cities architecturally, it is humanly wonderful too. People talk easily to strangers, communication is very relaxed, especially in the city's innumerable pubs, and the Irish have neither the aloofness of the English nor the arrogance of the French. I felt stirrings of my Celtic roots there: I felt at ease and unlonely. As my ancestors were Protestant rather than Catholic, I presume they must originally have come to Ireland from Scotland, and in both Ireland and Scotland I felt a kind of belonging I never felt in England. In one of my more recent books, *At Home and Abroad*, I tried to explore this sense of kinship and shared Celtic identity.

If you look at the book you will see some interesting parallels. For instance, I juxtaposed an Irish woman and her husband sitting in their kitchen with a South Island couple sitting in their kitchen. You would swear that not only do they eat the same sort of meals and have the same sort of conversations, but that the women have gone to the same dressmakers and hairdressers. Throughout Ireland I kept on having such stabs of recognition. So that's why we paint our houses all colours of the rainbow – that's what they do too! Patterns of relating, patterns of socialising, patterns of child-rearing have all persisted, at least in part, through generations and through distance.

My travels and explorations at that time were not confined to the British Isles. Keep in mind that New Zealand in the fifties and sixties, when I was growing up, was a pretty claustrophobic place. To me, as a university student, it had seemed to be a society closed in on itself, smug and intolerant, locked into a kind of endless Sunday afternoon. I had got away and I was determined to experience different ways and ideas, as well as different places. I hitch-hiked vast distances through Europe: up to Scandinavia, down through Spain and Portugal to Morocco, through the Low Countries, and France and Germany. I was not so much interested in ruins and art, or architecture and scenery, but in people – the way they did things, the way they looked at life, the cultural ties that bound them. I had some salutary experiences in coming to terms with my own prejudices and confronting my own stereotypes. For instance, I didn't at first much like the Germans (keep in mind that I was born in 1944), but then when I was cold, hungry and nearly penniless, a German fisherman rescued me from the side of the road, took me home to his family for a gigantic meal, schnapps and a warm bed, and was simple human kindness personified.

The most 'alien' of the countries I visited at that time was Morocco, and there too I relearned the simple truth that we are all, for good or ill, human. Morocco literally blew my mind – and not just because kif was freely available. I stayed in a very cheap hotel in the old Arab quarter and could easily find my way round its narrow windy streets in daylight because doors and shutters were open and you could see down passageways and through courtyards and so on. However, one night I was out happily walking with some Arab guys and without explanation the police arrested us and bundled us into their van and off to the police station. That was an eye-opener. There was not too much regard for the niceties of police procedures, nor basic human rights. Eventually a senior policeman who spoke some English showed faint curiosity about my plight and asked for my passport. It was back at the hotel, so he said I had half an hour to get it and bring it back. It was dark and I realised that with doorways and shutters closed I now had no idea how to find the hotel, nor was I having much success in explaining my difficulty to anyone. Finally a blind man with a white stick understood my quandary and led me unerringly to the hotel and back to the police station. Somehow that incident seemed to me to have an almost biblical significance. 'And the blind shall show you the way' sort of thing. When I got back to the police station the English-speaking officer showed only cursory interest in the passport, and simply warned me not to walk out with Arabs after dark. I'm not sure whether he was concerned for my safety or theirs.

Throughout all these travels and adventures I was unencumbered by a camera. I think I had to teach myself to see before I could teach myself to record what I saw. Although my father had been a professional photographer I did not really take much interest in it while I was growing up, and he certainly made no effort to recruit me to his craft. In many ways I taught myself the fundamentals in London when I got a job with a magazine called *International Times* in 1967. Despite its apparently orthodox title, it was a very unorthodox magazine, in fact a kind of precursor for *Oz*. They wanted me not just to write about demonstrations in London and Paris (mainly for racial equality or against America's involvement in Vietnam) but to get pictures of them too. I spent endless hours experimenting in a darkroom and endless rolls of film experimenting with my £10 camera. I learned by trial and error, and by always looking for the truth I wanted to capture and convey.

I started life as a practising photographer and as a married man at about the same time. My wife, Dinah, was also from New Zealand and also getting her Overseas Experience. Our first joint adventure was three months in the Greek Isles. On that trip I did take a camera, and plenty of black and white film, and really attempted to explore and capture the life of those around us. It was a simple peasant life in many ways, with ancient rhythms, but it was endlessly fascinating visually. We explored Crete and Rhodes and all the well-known tourist spots, but for me the most memorable part of the trip was the month we stayed in a village on a tiny island called Pserimos, near Kos. Most of the young men were away working as sponge divers, so the village was full of older people, pregnant women and children. We swam and slept and took our meals in a bar made of driftwood and cardboard right on the beach. It was usually grilled fish with something like tomatoes and cucumber from the village garden, but it was always absolutely delicious. Sometimes we paid for it, and sometimes they just shrugged and seemed not to be bothered to collect their money. Once a week the priest and his wife gave us a meal. (In the Orthodox church priests may marry so long as they do not aspire to become bishops.) They made an effort always to make this a special meal for us, and usually wrung the neck of a rabbit or a fowl with graphic accompanying gestures. The only language we had in common was the remnants of my schoolboy Latin. I'd never imagined it could be so useful.

Another trip we did together that I should mention was back to Cornwall. We rented a cottage so that I could recuperate from hepatitis, and we basically spent six months reading in front of a fire. One thing about that time, however, sticks particularly in my mind. The family who rented us the cottage had a Frances Hodgkins painting. She had been a friend of friends of theirs, and had spent some time in Cornwall. They loved their painting, wanted to talk about it and were (politely) surprised when we seemed to know so little of our own culture and literature. We were, I'm afraid to say, typical of our generation. Apart from Mansfield and Baxter we could barely name any New Zealand writers, yet we had studied literature at university and were quite well read in English (and Irish) novels and poems. About New Zealand paintings or music we knew even less than about New Zealand literature. We realised much of our education had been about the far side of the world, and we felt a kind of nakedness or shame in the face of this nice Cornish farming couple.

Well, I had had five years based in London by this time. I had turned my hand to innumerable jobs, had done a tremendous amount of travel, and had mastered the rudiments of what was to become my life's work, photography. Then a great change. Dinah became pregnant, and we both decided we wanted our child to be New Zealand-born and to enjoy a New Zealand childhood. In immigration terms we could have stayed indefinitely in London as Dinah's father was English-born, but we didn't even bother to discuss returning at length. We had good friends, good jobs and a good life, but we both instinctively wanted to go home to have our child. We did a farewell tour of Europe in a battered car we simply left at Milan airport, and flew out to the Antipodes.

Coming back was a real culture shock and at first we felt almost foreign. We stayed initially with my wife's sister in

Remuera, and I can remember a panicky feeling of desolation: those suburban footpaths and roads were so wide and deserted. Where were all the people? The landscape was empty. The other immediate and automatic response to New Zealand, even if you are not a photographer, is to marvel at the clarity of the atmosphere and the brightness of the light. You realise that your acuity of vision in Europe has been permanently blurred by atmospheric pollution or prolonged winters.

We did the correct New Zealand thing for any young couple expecting their first baby and bought our first house, in Ponsonby. When asked to transfer our telephone number from Remuera to Ponsonby the telephonic bureaucrat said, 'No one ever moves from Remuera to Ponsonby.' (And I had fondly imagined New Zealand to be classless!) But we did move from Remuera to Ponsonby – it was all we could afford. It had, however, what we believed every New Zealand child's birthright to be: a lawn to play on, trees to climb, and plenty of sunshine.

Since coming back in 1970 I have taken the business of being a New Zealander much more seriously and self-consciously than I did when I was young. I have read our books, looked at our movies and plays, sought out our painters and architects, and tried to empathise with Maori cultural aspirations just as I had formerly tried to respond to varieties of Europeanness. The Maori renaissance is something to view with pride rather than anxiety, I feel. Only when two peoples and two cultures feel at ease together in this land will we be able to look our past and our future in the eye.

The realisation of how profoundly I had changed in my feelings for this place only became really apparent when we returned to England as a family for a year in 1984. My wife and I had work to do, and the two boys, Jake and Keir (then ten and twelve), attended local schools in Greenwich. We were all busy and happy enough, but at the end of that year we all wanted to come home. A turning point for my youngest son Keir came when they were making banana milkshakes at school. He asked, 'Where are the bananas?' and was horrified to be ridiculed with the answer 'You don't use a banana, silly, you use banana flavouring.'

A turning point for me was being sent a copy of *the bone people*. The grey English rain was dripping on grey English houses and I was reading about the sea and the shore, about the kai moana and the bush, about solitude and silence and how people live with their landscape and are shaped by it. I thought, 'What the hell am I doing here?' When Dinah read the book she said, 'You should do a book with Keri Hulme'. And I did – *Homeplaces*.

I still travel a lot in the course of my work, in Australia and Europe, as well as within New Zealand itself. But wherever and whenever I go, New Zealand is where I want to live. The closed society of the 1950s is gone. I can now get coffee from anywhere in the world, see movies or buy books, magazines and compact discs from anywhere, and television shows me all the world's news just as soon as it shows it to anyone. The sense of apartness and distance is now diminished for young New Zealanders. The ones I know still want to see the world, but they do not have the same sense of claustrophobia and urgency as my generation did. I can walk down Karangahape Road and eat Vietnamese, Lebanese, Mexican or whatever cuisine takes my fancy. We have joined the global village.

My work now is mainly books. I occasionally exhibit in photographic galleries, but really I'm happier with my photographs in a book where they keep each other company, where you turn the pages, and where they tell a story. Each photo has to live by itself, but in reality they are always part of a sequence, and the sequence is more than the sum of its parts. I still enjoy exploring this country, and am coming to appreciate it more and more. I'm not just interested in chocolate-box beauty: that has been done to death. One must see and show without sentimentality.

If you look at my book *The South Island of New Zealand: From the Road* you will see that I was interested in characters, and what people have wrought, quite as much as I was interested in the marvels of the landscape. I quite understand why some primitive people will not allow themselves to be photographed for fear that their souls will be stolen. That is precisely what I try to do – to capture the essence of ordinary lives – and the people I portray in that book seem to epitomise important aspects of what it means to be a New Zealander. There is something quite frightening, in fact, about the South Island. It is so empty. My photographs show that frightening emptiness, and also how people assert themselves in the face of it. They build their tiny banks as imitation Greek temples, or they paint their houses magenta or peacock blue. If only I had a crate of those books under the bed I'd be rich. They are now a collector's item. The other day I saw one was auctioned in Dunbar Sloane's for $600.

People and places do things to each other, and in my photographs I hope to show that truth. Shakespeare knew that all the world's a stage, and we are all players on that stage. We have no other stage to play on. My photographic characters are players in the drama of New Zealand. They represent something about our collective life. When I photograph the Irish in Ireland it is the same. I'm not even fully conscious of what I'm doing, but increasingly my work is showing the inseparability of people and places. I know it is not yet politically correct for Pakeha to claim to be tangata whenua here in Aotearoa, but certainly for many of us, I believe, it is already emotionally correct. We know we want to be nowhere else. This is my country. Exploring it visually, and sharing my explorations with others, is my life's work. I have no other country and no other task.

# Ending the Colonial Cringe

## Richard Mulgan

Whether to live in New Zealand or England was an issue from the very beginning. My mother was English and my father a New Zealander. I was born in England but brought to New Zealand as a baby. My earliest childhood memories are of wartime Wellington, particularly of York Bay, Wellington Harbour and Eastbourne, of cabbage trees and Norfolk pines. There are many New Zealanders who came here with their parents to settle and who cannot remember their birthplace. The learnt fact of having been born on the other side must always mark a difference for the settler child, a potential for one day regaining the lost nationality and, at the same time, a blemish on one's claim to be a true New Zealander.

But we had not, at that stage, come to settle. Our time in New Zealand was a wartime expedient, a haven for my mother and myself until the war ended and we presumably resumed our life overseas. My father's death in the last months of the war did not alter that presumption. There was little to keep my mother here and so, at the age of five, after two terms of school, I was returned to England and my birthplace, Oxford. I entered an English school with the wrong accent and the wrong raincoat. New Zealand seemed likely to become nothing more than an early and increasingly irrelevant interlude in my life.

But my mother and I had already met another New Zealander making the academic pilgrimage to Oxford. In due course, to my great and lasting satisfaction, he became my stepfather. Unlike my father, he was not to be drawn into the life of expatriate exile. Just before my ninth birthday, which I was to miss crossing the international dateline, we sailed back again through the Panama Canal (destined to become an invaluable topic for school talks) and once more into Wellington Harbour, en route to a life in South Auckland. Once again, a new school with the wrong accent and the wrong raincoat.

The next decade was, in many ways, more settled as I progressed through the rest of primary, then intermediate and secondary school and on to university in Auckland. But the idea of where to live was still not fully resolved. My late father's English employers had offered his widow a benefit much valued in a society where good education costs money – financial support for her son's education. This included the guarantee of a place at my father's old Oxford college and financial support while I studied there. In the immediate post-war years, it must be remembered, the meritocratic assumptions of the Butler Education Act and the 11-plus examination had not yet fully hit the English universities. Entrance to Oxford and Cambridge could still be a matter of money and knowing the right people. It was quite natural for a five-year-old to be given a place. Thus, throughout my school and university days in New Zealand, the eventual prospect of a return to Oxford always lay before me. There was no doubt that I would make the journey myself, only about whether I would return in the end. Whether to be English or a New Zealander in nationality remained an open question for a while.

My two grandmothers, both powerful and determined matriarchs, competed over my future. My mother's English mother – she and my aunt had joined us in New Zealand soon after our return – hoped that an Oxford education might return me to the English professional class to which she belonged. My father's New Zealand mother pressed on me the need to identify with her pioneer roots and those of my grandfather. In the end it was the New Zealand side that won. Some time during my school years I became clearly convinced that New Zealand was my home. Those first memories of York Bay and my New Zealand grandparents had obviously been important. So too, perhaps, was the fact that I was my father's surviving child. But to be a New Zealander rather than English was still for me an act of choice and personal identification. For many of my friends who were born of New Zealand parents and had spent all their years here, there could be no option. The fact of choice implies an inevitable contingency and insecurity in the identification. I was always vulnerable to the anti-pommy put-down, the jeering at the odd anglicism in my speech or at my alien place of birth. Such insecurity may reveal itself in a certain over-enthusiasm for the assumed identity, the excessive zeal of the convert, to which I have probably always been prone.

Whatever our nationality, however, the journey to Britain was one that most of my friends and contemporaries expected or hoped to make themselves. England was very much part of our consciousness, and our experience was incomplete until we had visited it. The need to get to London was not so much part of a general urge to travel, the need for OE, as it was to become known. It was a need to visit the centre of our own world. The bond between New Zealanders (and here we are talking almost exclusively of Pakeha New Zealanders) and Britain was not only much stronger but also much more exclusive than it has since become. No one, for instance, as far as I remember, ever contemplated visiting Australia. Indeed, I had travelled round the world several times before I eventually went there in my early thirties. North America and Asia were simply more or less exotic stepping stones on the way there or the way back.

It is hard now to imagine the degree of cultural dependence on England in the fifties. Our newspapers gave great space to British news. Radio news, apart from a brief daily bulletin, was dominated by the BBC. When the Attlee Government was defeated by Churchill in 1951, I remember someone saying that that was a more important election for New Zealand than our own contest between National and Labour. When Britain invaded Suez in my last year at school, many of us assumed that we too might soon be at war and might be forced to fight as our fathers and grandfathers had done. 'Where Britain goes, we go' was not rabid jingoism but a straightforward expression of a self-evident assumption.

Interest in things English was naturally higher in our own household where my mother and her relations talked often of their times there. Many English friends and acquaintances, fellow expatriates, came to the house. But the interest in England was not confined to the recent immigrants. My parents' friends tended to be interested in books and the arts, and here, whether British-born or New Zealand-born, England, especially the cultural life of London, was pre-eminent. We took the *New Statesman*, which was read mainly for the book section and the theatre, film and music reviews. The front half, on British and international politics from a left-wing perspective, was later to help stir my growing interest in political ideas. The other treasured reading was the occasional copies of British Sunday papers passed on from more fortunate or affluent homes. Again these were read for the London reviews, and most of the arts-minded visitors to our house would have a view on the respective merits of the London reviewers, C.A. Lejeune and Dilys Powell, Harold Hobson or Kenneth Tynan. We had *Time* magazine as well, but the knowledge and interest in the American scene was never as intimate or involved as that with the English. This interest in the metropolis, it must be stressed, was not a sign of disaffection with New Zealand. True, there were some of our more disgruntled expatriate friends who complained about what they saw as the insularity of New Zealand and looked back to England with longing and regret. But those who felt settled here and were keen to see an independent cultural life develop in New Zealand also shared the same perspective.

My grandfather, my father's father, was a case in point. After our return to New Zealand, I made regular visits to my grandparents still living in the place of my earliest childhood memories, York Bay. My grandfather had spent all his life in New Zealand, except for one visit to Britain in the twenties. Much of his life was spent writing about New Zealand, its history and literature. His autobiography he called with pride and satisfaction, *The Making of a New Zealander*. Yet he was vitally interested in things English. He shaved every morning to the BBC News and looked forward to Sunday mornings and Sam Pollock's 'Newsletter from Britain'. He followed the fortunes of the English cricket team avidly. Though their regular triumphs over New Zealand might be treated with some mixed feelings, there could be no doubt about the rapture he felt when Statham and Tyson routed the Australians. It was as if we had done it ourselves. My grandfather was a passionate anglophile, never accepting any of the criticisms my mother, who was genuinely English, might make of the country of her birth. Tennyson, that most English of poets, was his favourite poet after Shakespeare, and Handel's *Messiah* his favourite piece of music. Of course he represented an older generation – few of my parents' generation, let alone my own, were at ease with the title of his book about his visit to Britain, *Home – A Colonial's Adventure*. But though their view of England might be less rose-tinted, it still held their attention. There was little doubt that London was the centre of our world, in much the same way as it might be for someone living in Cornwall or the Hebrides.

These assumptions were reinforced when I entered the university. My interest at school had gravitated to languages and maths, subjects which one could learn as one went and which did not, like history and chemistry, require massive feats of memory. In the end, through the ruthless test of the university scholarship examination, my maths was proved to be no more than competent and I enrolled for a BA, concentrating (it was not yet 'majoring', still seen as an ugly Americanism) on Latin and Greek. Classics, after all, I understood to be one of the strengths of Oxford, for which I was still heading. People with Oxford connections were in awe of the Classics course, 'Greats', which took four years rather than the normal three for the undergraduate BA and was supposed to train one for any conceivable career. An added inducement was that my father had not done it and, according to my mother, wished he had. I was always, I suspect, looking for opportunities to score points against his oppressive record.

By this stage, most of my university friends were arts students. Those who had chosen professional careers in law, accounting, medicine or engineering disappeared down town or went to other universities. Scientists put on white coats and lived in their laboratories. University life for us centred on the library and the cafeteria, in varying proportions. We had postponed a definite choice of career, but many, if we were doing well enough, looked to an academic career as a distant though highly desirable possibility. The great passport to this career was an overseas scholarship and Oxford and Cambridge still the preferred destinations. I was in the enviable and envied position of having my scholarship guaranteed, a source of embarrassment alongside friends who had still to make their way. The least I could do was to make an effort to deserve it in my eyes and theirs. And so shame encouraged an already existing thought that being an academic might be quite an interesting and enjoyable way to spend one's life.

The Classics Department at Auckland University shared the common preoccupation with England. The senior members of staff were New Zealanders with Oxbridge degrees, apart from Professor Edward Blaiklock, who had been forced by the Depression to choose between marriage and going to Cambridge. He claimed never to have regretted his choice, though we were not so sure. At any rate, in the economically booming post-war period it was not a choice that we ourselves would be forced into. The objects of admiration and ambition were those who had gone through the department and on to Oxbridge. Their names were often mentioned. The pinnacle of pinnacles were those who had not only gone but stayed. Highest by far was Sir Ronald Syme, Professor of Roman History at Oxford, probably New Zealand's greatest ever scholar. Stories were still told of how in the 1920s, before he had finally graduated, he had come to Auckland from Victoria in Wellington to be an assistant lecturer. He had thus lectured to his fellow students and marked his own terms exams. Syme made one of his periodic returns to New Zealand while we were students and gave some lectures. We were struck by how anglicised and mannered he was, seeming more English than the English. (Later, when I heard him again in Oxford, he appeared, in a different context, to be cultivating a slightly raffish air, and was certainly not trying to hide his colonial origins.) But there were others too, besides Syme, ex-Auckland classicists such as George Cawkwell and A.H. McDonald, who were fellows at Oxford and Cambridge, and clearly at the top of their particular profession.

Thus when I set off for Oxford I was following a well-worn path, which could lead either to permanent success abroad or a return to New Zealand, a question as yet unsettled. The final act before leaving was to obtain a passport. I was eligible for either a United Kingdom or a New Zealand passport but was determined to have a New Zealand one, as an affirmation of my national identification. This proved to be harder than expected. My length of residence in the country – fourteen of my twenty years – did not count. Descent and place of birth were all, and I needed evidence of my father's birth and marriage to my mother. My parents' marriage certificate had been lost in the upheavals of wartime and a certified copy from Somerset House in London would take months to obtain. The helpful officials in the passport office in Wellington suggested more than once that it would be much easier for me to go down the road to the British High Commission where a United Kingdom passport could be issued in a matter of days. I was angered and humiliated that my country would not recognise my citizenship. In the end, I was given a temporary New Zealand passport for six months, to be extended to the full term on sight of my parents' marriage certificate. This would give me time to get to London and obtain a copy for myself, which in due course I did. In retrospect, this appears as a decision of considerable bureaucratic flexibility and sensitivity. But it hurt at the time.

Oxford was far from alien. I remembered its geography from before and had picked up an acquaintance with many of its arcane ways and customs from family and friends. To begin with, my social life centred on old Auckland friends and other overseas graduate students, such as American Rhodes scholars, of whom there were a number in my college – a very interesting group, chosen by rather more enlightened criteria than New Zealand Rhodes scholars of my time. We all had something in common, being new to the country and slightly older than our English fellow students. But I soon came to know some of my English contemporaries as well, indeed better. I had the good fortune of doing the undergraduate Classics course from the beginning. I had a BA from New Zealand but school leavers from the best English schools had been learning Latin and Greek for longer than I had. There was some catching up for me to do. However, I was used to the freedom of university life and to organising my time, and before long I had read as much Latin and Greek literature as my contemporaries, though I never acquired their amazing fluency in translating English into the ancient languages.

Being part of the Classics intake (there were nine in my year in my college) placed me firmly in the mainstream of college life and I was treated as an equal and no more an outsider than most of the others. New Zealanders have the background to negotiate the English class system with relative ease, being accepted at all levels. Many of my friends had come only a short distance geographically to Oxford, from the Midlands or the North, but they had more difficulty than I with the residual snobbishness of Oxford. Oxford in the sixties was largely meritocratic in composition, both teachers and students. These were the years when Harold Wilson, the grammar school scholarship boy, knocked Harold Macmillan and Alec Douglas-Home off their aristocratic perch. A northern accent was a positive advantage. Alan Bullock, the biographer of Hitler and the head of Oxford's latest college, was said to have quickly relearned the strong Yorkshire accent that he had erased in his earlier years. But even then there were a few undergraduates who aspired to the languid aristocratic Oxford of Beerbohm and Waugh. Sitting one night at dinner next to one of them and attempting conversation, I asked where he had been to school. 'Charterhouse,' the reply. 'Where is Charterhouse?' I asked, in genuine ignorance. 'I don't think that joke's funny,' was the reply. I gave up. Another young buck once complained to me about the college's sad decline in its rowing. All the fault of the new concentration on brains – 'the place has become full of little chaps with big heads'. But these were a minority, marginalised among the dominant group of undergraduates who came from very different backgrounds, chosen on academic ability and potential and among whom I felt entirely at home. My accent no longer mattered and I had the right coat (a duffle coat, naturally, in those days). Oxford was in many ways an international community, as all universities are to a certain extent.

I also had introductions to a number of the New Zealand expatriates settled in Oxford, members of my father's generation who belonged to the class of famous New Zealanders overseas. Of most interest to me were their children, my contemporaries, who had lived the life that I would have lived myself had not the war intervened to rescue me. They were now fully integrated into the English professional class, having attended highly selective (and often expensive) schools, and were on their way to the sort of interesting careers that such education can purchase one in England. At the same time they witnessed a steady stream of New Zealand visitors and listened to their parents reminiscing about New Zealand, often in a highly romanticised way. One of them said to me that she felt cheated. If New Zealand was such a great place to grow up in, why had her parents denied her that opportunity? The stated reason was always that there was not the same type of interesting work for the fathers in New Zealand. But I felt that this was more of an excuse, that the expatriates were actually happy in their exile. Their professed attachment to New Zealand and the frequent claims that they would have returned if only there were suitable work was a form of self-deception. The romantic expatriates lived a lie.

After four years I completed my undergraduate years with First Class Honours in classical 'Mods' and 'Greats'. It had taken much hard work and some luck. I had scraped rather than sailed in. But the result was good enough to guarantee entry to an academic career. More important, it satisfied me that I had deserved my place at Oxford, however unjustly gained, and could once and for all step out of my father's shadow. I won a scholarship (in my own right at last) and started on postgraduate study. I had three years more in Oxford while I completed a postgraduate degree and had a year as an assistant lecturer. I was also married, to a New Zealander, and our first child was born.

By this time there was little doubt that we would return to New Zealand. The ambiguous life of the expatriate exiles was repellent. It might suffice for the childless scholar, like Ronald Syme, whose life was confined to the stateless community of the university. But a family made all the difference. To stay would

95

mean to settle, to identify with the English and deny, or at least walk away from, our New Zealand background. I also rejected the option of taking a first job in England, of gaining experience overseas and then hoping to return to a senior position, such as a professorship, in middle life. This was a familiar career path for New Zealanders with academic ambitions. But it was a risky option, because one might not get the job one wanted and might end up an expatriate exile by default. Besides, as far as children were concerned, as I knew myself, those first years were critical. Delaying our return till the children might be in their teens would deprive them of their chance to be New Zealanders. Also, like other New Zealand friends in Britain at the time who were thinking of an eventual career back home, I wanted to do something to reject the old assumption that true academic success was to go overseas and stay either permanently or until one could return at the top. Why should New Zealanders always assume that their ablest people lived elsewhere? Was this not one more instance of colonial cringe?

In the later sixties university jobs were not nearly as hard to get as they were to become. I had by this stage moved from Classics to Politics and there were vacant posts in Political Studies in almost all the universities. In the end, I went to Wellington, to the astonishment of Auckland friends. Victoria University, like any other New Zealand university of the time, was very different from Oxford. The system was less élitist and the students more varied in ability and age. The staff, on average, were not as able or well qualified. But the best students were as good as any anywhere and there were bright and well-informed colleagues with whom to exchange ideas and gossip. In spite of all my determination to remain a New Zealander and to return to live and work here, seven years in Oxford had imbued me with some of its metropolitan snobbery. I half expected that intellectual life would be comparatively dull in the colonial backwater. I was ashamed to notice in myself a certain surprise at the high level of academic ability and achievement on the part of both students and staff. I realised clearly for the first time the lie in complaints about New Zealand's insularity, which I had heard from the disgruntled expatriates in my childhood. This amounted to no more than a complaint that New Zealanders were less interested in England than the English were. New Zealanders were, in fact, the least insular of peoples and our universities the least insular of universities. Being away from the main intellectual centres forces us to look outwards, to keep *au fait* with the main overseas trends, both in Europe and North America. The curse of large metropolitan centres like Oxford is the delusion of self-sufficiency, the false belief that everything worth knowing and thinking about is known and thought within their own confines. That is the true and stultifying insularity.

Twenty-five years on, there is little to regret in that decision to return. New Zealand universities, with their greater openness to all comers and their general comparability of standing, serve their communities much better than élitist and hierarchical English universities serve theirs. I have had some very rewarding students to teach, not least among the mature second-chance students who are virtually absent from the British university system. Not only are they a delight to teach but their successful use of university retraining has been one of the most important avenues of equal opportunity, especially for women. There has also been time to do some writing and participate in the international academic dialogue. Study leave and conference travel allow one to keep up with what others are doing. Though they are part of their local communities, universities, like monasteries in the Middle Ages, are also members of an international community. In this respect, as far as one's work goes, there is less difference between living in England or North America and New Zealand than there might be in other jobs. We read many of the same books and debate many of the same theories. It seems too that the distances have been steadily diminishing. There is much less sense of intellectual exile among New Zealand academics, I suspect, than when I was a student. Moreover, there is much less absorption in England and Oxbridge. North America is now an equally important, probably more important, intellectual focus.

As for the ongoing experiment of European settlement in New Zealand, much has happened in the last quarter century and much of it for the better. True, we still underestimate our own abilities and accord excessive deference to overseas experts or the returning expatriate. Pakeha New Zealanders have had to face the growing recognition that the process of European colonisation which brought us here was unjust and indefensible. We also have to put up with being regularly told that we do not know who we are – a very mystifying claim. At least there can be no doubt that Pakeha New Zealanders are at home here and nowhere else. More worrying is the erosion of those distinctive aspects of New Zealand life which made it seem fairer and more comfortable than life in Britain or the US. I sometimes wonder whether if I were studying overseas now I would want to make the same decision to return. But this is a decision for each generation.

# Issues of Identity

## Paul Reeves

My family never had much to come or go on and for my father, who struggled with ill health, security was the really important issue. I used to watch him doing sums on the back of an envelope with an indelible ink pencil. The goal was to pay off the mortgage and buy a car. My father achieved both at about the same time as he died.

The search for security does funny things to our lives. Today if you lack capital you tend to find security in more children. Conversely, if you have capital you find security in more capital. My father was an exception. He had no capital and he had only two sons. But he was still driven by the desire for security. What he did was to choose my brother's first job by the pension it would offer after forty years of drudgery. My brother rebelled against that. No wonder he joined the Navy just as soon as he could.

By contrast, my mother fashioned my choices, and almost as an act of reparation I went to Wellington College, which for me was not an easy environment, and then on to Victoria University College, which I loved. There I found a freedom to explore choices and develop a personal discipline. In the first year I joined the Rugby Club, the second year I joined the Student Christian Movement, but subsequently I concentrated on rugby. I became acquainted with the back bar of the Midland Hotel. I read widely and my standard of dress was uniformly untidy.

The student body was just moving out of a period of intense political activity. Nevertheless, we watched awful Chinese films about the 1949 revolution and argued about the nature of the government intervention in the 1951 waterside strike.

My academic career has always been long on hard work and short on attainment. At Victoria I haunted the library and read everything, but the ultimate mark was not good. When I went to study for the priesthood at St John's College in Auckland I found that the standard was lower and the secret of success was a copy of the sub-warden's notes which reduced mystery to ten points. We lived a monastic routine of chapel four times a day and silence from 9.30 p.m. until the next morning. Women visitors were tolerated but never really welcomed. Most of the time I enjoyed it.

My mother was an active member of the Wellington Anglican Maori Pastorate and the Maori Women's Welfare League, and in the middle of 1957 I was approached by Mr Tipi Ropiha who had been an assistant secretary for Maori Affairs. Would I consider applying for the Sir Apirana Ngata Memorial Scholarship? Hugh Kawharu had gone to Oxford; so too had Charles Bennett, but he had withdrawn to become New Zealand High Commissioner in Malaysia. I got the impression that I was the last throw of the dice. Things were desperate.

But it was the challenge which shaped my life. Crudely speaking, could I accept a Maori scholarship without accepting the responsibility of discovering what it might mean to be a Maori? That question sat there and gnawed at me for years. A sociologist even used me as a case study. On the other hand, I was being offered a chance to go back to university for a second try, to study theology in an ancient university and to explore the wider world of England and Europe which up until then I had barely thought about.

By virtue of being ordained I had put myself into an authority structure in which the expectation was that you would obey your bishop. Later on when I became a bishop I realised just how mistaken I was in that expectation. It was 1959 and I was curate at St Francis' Church, Tokoroa, living in a small house with a minimum of furniture which included a radio, a table and a mattress on the floor. The scholarship did not come through easily and I even wrote to Walter Nash, the prime minister of the day. More to the point, he wrote back and wished me well. But I clearly remember the afternoon when I was sweeping out the parish lounge and Les Anderson, the vicar, appeared to say the bishop had been told by the prime minister that the scholarship was mine.

I had no sense of wanting to leave New Zealand to escape its provincialism, conservatism, or anything else. As a child of the Depression and the war years, my travelling had been severely limited. Most holidays I stayed home. Occasionally I travelled to Picton. In fact I had barely explored my own country. Apart from Picton and Nelson, the South Island was a mystery, and I had been no further north than Auckland. New Zealand was put on hold to be walked, driven and flown over at a later date.

The emotional ties with people were another matter. I used to hitch-hike from Tokoroa to Hamilton to spend time with Beverley, who had found a teaching position at Fairfield College. We were married before departing for England on the last voyage of the RMS *Rangitata*, that greyhound of the Pacific which on some days could summon up only five knots. Leaving my mother was a different story. She taught me that love requires a mother to let a son go. I am sure that the twists and turns of my career were already confusing her, but she had the serenity and the wisdom to let things happen.

I suppose there never was any doubt that we would return to New Zealand one day. In fact I had an understanding with the bishop that five years in England was my allotted span. I remember driving north out of Oxford to the small village of Merton. For years the vicar had been Henry Dewsbury Alves Major, a New Zealander and a modernist theologian who had even been tried for heresy in the 1920s. Major had died just before we reached England and we found his grave in a corner of the churchyard. His son had been killed in the war and there was a memorial to him in the church. I felt sad that a notable man who on his headstone was identified as a New Zealander had died and was buried so far from home. I did not want that for myself.

Except for the examination results, Oxford was a wonderful experience. The one-to-one relationship with a tutor to whom you read an essay each week was a challenge. Tutors were interesting people in themselves. One, who seemed to have a perpetual cold, dried out his handkerchief before the electric fire while I tried to concentrate on reading my essay. Another was said periodically to surprise his students by sitting beneath the table or on top of the wardrobe. Our landlady, aged seventy-nine, saw a man's face at the window while she was having a bath. She confessed that she did not know whether to be scared or flattered, but she still sent me out in my bare feet clutching a golf club to chase the intruder down the gravelled path.

There are scores of memories but Oxford was also a revelation. I realised I had gained entry to the university because I was an outsider and not many wanted to study theology. My New Zealandness got me in, not my brains. Students from English working-class backgrounds similar to mine often seemed to be screwed up emotionally. They found it hard to relate to where they came from, and they were uncertain if they commanded the respect of their contemporaries at Oxford. Probably they did not. I used to study at Pusey House, which was basically a library and a chapel staffed by a group of single clergy. I was even offered lodgings and had to tell them I was married. They looked at me with a mixture of disbelief and sorrow.

Leaving New Zealand actually introduced me to New Zealand. I saw it from a distance, talked about it, read William Pember Reeves (no relative, alas), F.L.W. Wood, and the poetry of Rex Fairburn and Allan Curnow. Do you know Fairburn's letter in which he says, 'I have an increasing conviction that I shouldn't be able to stay away from New Zealand indefinitely. Men are not free. They are bound by fate to certain things and lose their souls in escaping. This natural scene in England is lovely but I have no sympathy with it. I had rather be beside a smelly New Zealand creek'? The Maori side lay dormant. That worried me a bit, and I knew I would have to face up to it at some time in my life. My Pakeha antecedents all come from England but I never followed them up. There were no distant cousins to call on. In fact I did not explore the rather tangled

English family tree until I had become immersed in whakapapa and, dare I say it, unclaimed monies and succession to land titles.

We loved Oxford and Oxford people. The two Miss Spooners were typical. Daughter and niece of the famous Dr Spooner, and committed socialists, they entertained widely and were wont to serve up burnt carrots on exquisite Georgian silver. But it would have been self-indulgent to stay in Oxford, so we went and spent two and a half years in Lowestoft, an East Anglian fishing port. If you are looking for charm and beauty, don't go to Lowestoft. Its one saving grace is that it gives you access to the lovely counties of Norfolk and Suffolk. Beverley has always been able to turn a necessity into a virtue and create a wonderful and colourful environment out of very little. By that I mean a rug thrown over an old chair, a front door painted yellow, a box which becomes a seat, a table which has seen better days. I recall that a lady gave us the bed she had been born on. It had a horse-hair mattress and was very hard. In Lowestoft we lived in two houses: one was indescribably filthy, the other was freezing cold. But at a certain time in your life you can immerse yourself in the process of making do. We did that in England. We buried a child in the churchyard at Lowestoft and the thought of leaving him so far from the homeland he never knew even now makes me sad.

Time moved on and the understood date for returning to New Zealand drew nearer. I wanted to teach theology and one part of me said that if I could not do that in New Zealand then perhaps I should not go home. That was not how the bishop saw it. When I met him at New Zealand House in London he had just dropped his overcoat which had a bottle of whisky stuffed in one of the pockets. He lost both the whisky and for a while his normal cheerful disposition. The bishop led me to a travel agency in Trafalgar Square and stood over me; meanwhile I booked a passage back to New Zealand for the three of us (daughter Sarah was a recent and very welcome arrival).

Can I say that I was reluctant to return home? The truth was England had become familiar. My reading diet was the *Guardian*, the *New Statesman*, and the *Church Times*. The great world events were all around me. The issue was not simply nuclear testing but whether it would be our child who might be adversely affected by the presence of Strontium-90 in the milk. Politicians were interesting. When, like John Profumo, they fell from grace, they did it with a certain style. Field Marshal Montgomery and the retired Archbishop of Canterbury were stomping the country. I enjoyed the intensity of the debate. It was an age of satire, we were told, and suddenly on BBC Television David Frost appeared.

To return home seemed to be a long voyage away from an exciting environment, with no guarantee that there would be much excitement when I got back. I was even a little scared. The Maori dimension remained to be explored. A small Taranaki parish where the bishop was determined to send me meant living in the country, and I had never done that before. It meant re-establishing relationships, some of which I had been quite happy to deal with at a distance.

There is a sense in which it is easier to stay away from New Zealand and feel bad about it than to return home and deal with it. To my surprise I enjoyed country living. Sarah had a lawn rather than the landing at the top of a staircase to play on. Farmers work where they live and I enjoyed meeting them. I enjoyed being judged on my merits. The community generally responded readily to what I had to offer and suddenly I found myself to be a successful young vicar. A Fellow from my Oxford college came to stay and told me one night that it must be hard ministering to such simple people. That made me quite indignant. I was conscious that I was a New Zealander and he was expressing a viewpoint that belonged somewhere else, in another country.

Taranaki is littered with signs of Maori habitation. On my days off I explored pa sites and traced out the fortifications. I read about Maori-Pakeha conflicts in the 1860s, I visited the decaying but enormously impressive Parihaka Pa, and suspected that the people there knew more about me than they had revealed. It was the immediacy and accessibility of history which took my breath away. There were one or two old people who could remember events which the professional historians were assessing in scholarly articles and books.

What shook me was to meet my Taranaki relatives and to discover that, by descent, family connections and the ownership of
land, I was intimately connected to this history which had seized
me. The relationship with relatives began tentatively. I buried
an uncle; I went to Manukorihi Pa, Waitara; an aunt wanted to
see and hold our daughter. Years later these were the same people who supported me when I became the Governor-General. I
listened to what another uncle said about Te Whiti o Rongomai,
Tohu Kakahi and Parihaka itself. Someone gave me a copy of my
whakapapa and it fascinated me. I spent hours puzzling it out
and worked on my connections to Waikanae, Wellington and
Waikawa, as well as Taranaki. Identity is both given and
claimed. There is a subtle interplay between the individual and
the group. It is not a matter of them liking you or not liking you.
Rather, the person returning to his Maori roots must locate himself within both the history and the hopes of those who are
becoming his family, his people, his tribe. This is a long, com-
plicated and still-evolving story, but sufficient to say that issues
of identity and personhood began to be addressed. I felt comfortable with being a Maori; it was something to explore, not to
run away from.

The lower West Side of Manhattan, they say, is coming up.
Well, I am glad that I was not here when it was going down.
Everything seems like the re-run of an old movie. As in 1959,
so in 1991 we chose to leave New Zealand for what seemed
good and compelling reasons. Only this time we are thirty-two
years older, with daughters in Auckland, Honolulu and
London, an aged parent and a feeling that we belong in New
Zealand as we belong nowhere else. We even gave our dog
away. But here we are in New York, the apartment is comfortable but we suffer on two counts: we can't turn the central
heating down, and 21st Street right behind us is at its liveliest
and noisiest around 3 a.m. I relate to the United Nations which
labours to make sense of what Dag Hammarskjold called 'the
one world we have created before we were ready for it'. In the

meantime the garbage piles up on 21st Street and people pick it over in search of aluminium cans. We don't feel at ease in this city. The question of what we do next returns more frequently the older we get. The choices now have to be made within the current economic and employment circumstances, the claims of family and the suspicion that job-wise I am not exactly hot property. Suddenly the future seems more uncertain than when we left England in 1964 to return to New Zealand. There is no bishop to tell me what to do.

Great Whale River is an untidy settlement on the edge of Hudson Bay. The blanket of snow and ice and the stillness of it all reminds me of the old radio advertisement of my childhood for Buckley's Canadiol Cough Mixture when the wolf howled and the voice said, 'Throw another log on the fire.' In this part of Northern Canada the sea is frozen over until May. But now a great inland expanse of water has been created by Stage One of the James Bay Hydro Development Project, and if Stage Two proceeds a further area of land almost the size of France will be flooded. I have come to spend time with the Cree and the Inuit people who look remarkably like some of my Taranaki relatives. They greet us warmly at the airport and that means shaking hands with about thirty people. I am staying with Maggie and Andrew Natacheguan, a Cree couple who, when the weather warms up, will leave their home for the camp where they will hunt and fish. They speak no English and I have no Cree, so we spend a lot of time making exaggerated movements and excessive sounds in the hope that we can communicate over basic things like where is the lavatory and what time is dinner? It is awkward, I am feeling a long way from home and then I spot on the wall a picture of the Bushwhackers, an enormously successful pair of wrestlers who originated from Wellington. I could have kissed them. Judging from their picture that would have been an act of the will, for their days of beauty are well and truly behind them. Well, so are mine, but I am glad to see them. It is a silly little incident.

> . . . Things fall apart,
> the centre cannot hold,

wrote W.B. Yeats, and in the past few years New Zealand has been brushed by a spirit of hopelessness. The confidence of 1959 and 1964 was born out of a sense that we could relate to the world on our terms. But now times have changed. Economic recovery when it comes won't mean jobs for all. Some people may never work for wages. If we lose the middle group which is neither very rich nor very poor it will be the democratic process which will suffer. Power will flow to those who have the resources. The times, as always, are critical.

My own choices remain to be made. New Zealand has fashioned me and the radical thing would be to pack up, return home and see what happens. And yet I hesitate. It is a tougher situation this time around.

# The Circle Is Complete

## Patricia Rianne

One of my earliest memories is the first time I danced on stage when I was four years old with cousin Prue. I was one of a group of fairies dancing to the music of Tchaikovsky's 'Sugar Plum Fairy' in a concert organised by one of my aunts. What stands out in my mind is not the excitement of performing on stage but the little bouquet made of liquorice allsorts which each of us received at the end of the concert.

I come from a close-knit family. My father, Leo, the sickly one of twelve children, was born at Rongokakaka, near Eketahuna in the Wairarapa. He was a 'self-made' man, having started work as a stamp and errand boy in the Department of Social Security in Wellington during the Depression. Over the years he was promoted to more responsible positions, achieving registrar status. My mother, Betty, was from Palmerston North, a dancer and teacher of dance before her marriage, and a nutrition and exercise fanatic. My parents were living in Paremata when I was born prematurely, while my mother was visiting her family in Palmerston North. Five years later my only brother Christopher was born and from the first time I saw him he became a most cherished friend. Although we were to be parted for many years we always remained close.

From a very early age the importance of health and exercise was impressed upon me by my mother, who regularly swam, played golf and tennis. My mother was my first ballet teacher, coaching me almost from the cradle so that when, at the age of six, I was enrolled for my first formal lessons at the Judy Lewis School of Dance in Naenae, I slipped into the discipline of classes and practice without difficulty.

With my mother's encouragement and support, ballet became first and foremost in my life. Throughout my childhood I took part in dance competitions during school holidays, with considerable success. I was slightly puzzled by the whole process of performance and competition. On the one hand we were being trained as performers and expected to go on stage and show off our skills for which the best received prizes, and on the other hand any child who skited off stage was frowned upon. As my career developed I learnt that competition is an integral part of performing as the dancer strives to perfect performance.

During my secondary school years we lived in Wanganui, where I attended Sacred Heart College. My mother, believing I had the potential to make a career in dance, watched closely over my development and encouraged and supported me at every step. Each day I cycled several miles to school, afterwards practised tennis and then went to ballet and piano lessons before going home. My evenings were taken up with ballet and piano practice and homework. My schedule meant I had little time for the usual teenage pursuits, but it never occurred to me that it should be otherwise. Despite my total involvement with ballet I managed to achieve high marks in sixth form art, English and history, and was captain of the college tennis team. That year I was invited to Wellington during the Christmas school holidays to take part in the Wellington City Ballet's production of *Children of the Mist*. I was chosen to dance the leading role at the matinée, my first experience of being centre stage with the responsibility this involved. This led to an invitation to attend the New Zealand Ballet Summer School at the end of that year. At the Summer School we danced all day, rehearsing for performances under the direction of Poul Gnatt, the company's founder. I was desperately shy and still remember being overwhelmed to see so many good dancers gathered together battling for recognition.

At the end of Summer School I was offered a one-year contract to go on tour with the New Zealand Ballet. That year was one of the happiest of my life. We did performances from one end of New Zealand to the other, an experience which stood me in good stead and helped me develop the stamina needed to survive abroad. I learnt about hard work and the joy of performing. I also learnt to cope with the displays of bitchiness which sometimes erupted because of the stress of living in close confines and the competitive struggle for recognition. I recall the pleasure of watching and learning from older and more experienced dancers whom I gazed at wide-eyed, trying to emulate them. Years later I was credited with the ability quickly to adopt differing styles and a skill in mimicry and character acting which, I am sure, resulted from that early habit of observing other dancers. New Zealand Ballet at that time was like a happy family, but like any family, it had its dramas. I cherish many memories of that tour: the kind and hospitable billets in every centre we played, the packing and unpacking of the 'blue boxes' which contained everything to do with performance, the Volkswagen we travelled in, and the smell of grease paint. I remember dancing at parties, teaching myself to smoke because everyone else did and it was considered elegant, and the joy of being taken off ironing because I put the hot iron through Mr Gnatt's dragonfly outfit just before a performance.

During that year I made up my mind to go to England. I was constantly being told that in order to develop as a dancer I would have to go overseas to study and gain experience. Dance in New Zealand was still in its infancy and the New Zealand Ballet was the only professional company in the country. Being based on the traditional European art form, the development of dance in New Zealand relied heavily on people with experience acquired overseas. Encouraged by Gloria Young and Graeme Pickering, the mother and father of the company, I became convinced that going abroad was the right thing to do.

I saved every penny I could, and in November 1961 auditioned for a New Zealand Government bursary. Every second year one bursary was offered to an aspiring dancer to study at the Royal Ballet School in London. Each hopeful applicant performed two dances before a fearsome panel of judges and was then subjected to an in-depth interview. Although I had always been able to express myself through performance I was not very articulate. I had to fight back tears as the panel kindly asked me questions which seemed to have no purpose. I wanted to say, 'Please just give me the money and I'll prove I can do it', but my upbringing and shyness would never have allowed me to say anything so directly from the heart. All I wanted was to perform on stage; there I could lose myself in a fantasy world where I communicated through my dancing. I thought the interview would have ruined my chances of winning the bursary, so I was delighted to be a joint winner with Margaret Frost, another young dancer with the New Zealand Ballet. The only problem was that the money was to be shared, and I knew that my family, while giving me all the moral support I could wish for, were unable to help me financially.

My departure was traumatic. I was unprepared emotionally for the terrible wrench of leaving loved ones. In hindsight I was too young and lacked the skills to survive without the protection of family and friends. I was devastated, and experienced a loneliness I could not have anticipated. I still find it hard to think about that time in my life. The wall I built around me to protect myself never entirely disappeared until, as a sophisticated, experienced woman, I returned to the country of my birth twenty-six years later.

I left New Zealand on the *Fairsea* in January 1962 and was pleased to have Gray Malt as a travelling companion. He was another aspiring dancer who was later to make his mark as Gray Veredon, producer and choreographer. The journey lasted a testing six weeks. The constant round of food, drink and social flim-flam was relieved only by the ports of call, Singapore, Colombo, Aden and Port Said, through the Suez Canal to Naples and finally to Southampton. Such exotic places appealed to the romantic in me. Those first sights, smells, colours and sounds so different from home stayed with me long after I became a seasoned traveller.

Arriving in Southampton was a cultural and emotional shock. I found that London was many miles away from Southampton, necessitating a long train journey which was not included in my budget. The sudden realisation that I knew nobody was a frightening introduction to my new life. The smog-laden air, with snow falling intermittently out of low, leaden skies, echoed my misery. I had never been so cold and wanted only to cry. I yearned for 'my hills', the lovely shadowed Ruahines and Tararuas; thinking about them became my solace.

I found my way to London and the Royal Ballet School in Barons Court. I was told on arrival that I was in fact six months early, their school year being from September to June, not February to December as it is in New Zealand. Somehow this fact had never been communicated to me. I was given a list of places where I might find accommodation and after asking to leave my leather trunk in the office I went in search of a bed. I was shattered by the impersonal reception and was very aware that I was disrupting their schedules by arriving six months early. However, I found accommodation close to the school and was able to start classes almost immediately. The school was large, clinical and a conglomeration of 'heavenly bodies', all aspiring ballerinas. I was overwhelmed.

For one year and a term I attended the Royal Ballet School. When I was troubled I slept. I saved money from already inadequate funds so that I could go to the theatre, see the sights and take additional classes with private teachers away from the school. Those classes in particular were important to me. It was refreshing to get away from the claustrophobic atmosphere of the school and the self-absorption of my peers to work with the professional dancers who shared these classes. I wanted only to dance. At the school I found the constant analysis of technique frustrating. Only later did I appreciate the value of that excellent analytical training.

Money was a constant problem. I often went without food. My parents sent me boxes of New Zealand apples which, with gingernuts, cheddar cheese and black coffee, made up my entire diet for six weeks until I became ill with Bell's palsy. Luckily it was treated in time to prevent any permanent damage. Along with a small group of penniless students we cheated London Transport in order to get to Covent Garden Opera House, which we entered sometimes six to one ticket, thanks to standing room inside and a certain amount of ingenuity. To a 'country girl' it was all dreamlike. Finally when I did appear on that stage it was disappointing, but the reality of dreams is often so. (The Coliseum stage where I performed with Nureyev much later was huge and memorable, though I always had a soft spot for the homely Sadler's Wells. The Continental theatres were also impressive and so different from theatres in New Zealand, though no less hospitable.)

My English room-mate was older and had been brought up in Jamaica. Her family took me in on holidays with open arms long after Judi had gone to work in France, and I enjoyed my first very white Christmas from the cosy, homely interior of their Tudor country house.

My bursary was due to run out before the end of my time at the School, leaving me with one term without funds. A friend of my mother, Aileen Greaves, who was an opera and ballet lover, was a school teacher in London at the time and she offered to pay for my last term. The dancing teachers of Wanganui, in a singularly amazing gesture, put on a concert to raise funds for my support. The money, and in particular this expression of goodwill, assisted me more than I can say. The School then offered me the chance to continue for another year, but fate intervened. During the last term I was chosen as one of six 'extras' to take part in *Night Tryst,* a new work by Frederick Ashton, for the exquisite Svetlana Beriosova and handsome Donald MacCleary. Eighteen years later I danced at the Edinburgh Festival and toured England with these two lovely people.

My old flatmate Judi returned to the UK on holiday and we decided to go to Paris, she to audition, me to see the sights. It was my intention to stay on at School. As moral support I did the audition class with Judi and, in short, out of the sixty hopefuls, we were both soon rehearsing in Marseilles for a star-studded tour of Spain, southern France and Algeria. The company was the Ballet de l'Opéra de Marseilles, and the stars were all people out of picture books that I had at home. They included Colette Marchand, Jean-Paul Comelin, Milenko Banovich, Vassili Sulich, Ethéry Pagava, Janine Moran and Miskovitch. The training was exhausting but exhilarating. We often performed in open-air theatres at night. Large beetles, moths and bats flew

113

blindly into the lights and the dancers. During *Les Sylphides* one night, a large crawling thing landed on the bodice of a colleague while we were posed in statuesque positions. We watched mesmerised as it crawled over her bust towards the bare skin above her bodice. When it finally touched her skin, she fainted and had to be unceremoniously dragged into the wings.

We rehearsed over and over again. The director, fanatical about rehearsal, would continually shout, 'Once more!' and 'Full out without tiring yourselves!' As any athlete knows, it is impossible to work physically 'full out' without tiring yourself, but no one dared challenge the director and we worked until we were close to exhaustion. However, lunch breaks were lengthy affairs, in keeping with the tradition of the siesta. These provided the only relief from the gruelling schedule, and were often spent eating huge salades niçoise and cheese with red wine around a large table in a nearby café, with everyone talking excitedly at once. The French could not pronounce my surname properly, the y after r in Ryan causing the problem. To overcome the problem I eventually changed the spelling to Rianne. I became affectionately known as 'La petite Rianne du tout', which translates as 'little nothing', an endearment they thought amusing and charming. My time with this company was a drama-filled eighteen months; nothing seemed to happen without maximum noise and 'hype'. I loved it. We toured France with resident seasons in Marseilles and the Champs-Elysées in Paris.

In the summer of '63 I went to Cannes to do classes with the famous Rosella Hightower, and there I was offered a contract by director Freddie Franklin for Washington Ballet. At the same time I was offered the chance to return to New Zealand to dance the part of the token girl in *One in Five* by Ray Powell, as part of a national tour starring Alexander Grant in *Petrushka*. The chance to see my family and dance in New Zealand again was an opportunity I could not refuse. I stayed for ten months. During this time Russell Kerr, the New Zealand Ballet Company's artistic director, taught Jon Trimmer and me *Giselle* Act II which we performed on tour. In Kaikoura we received a 'rave review' in the local paper. I was so overwhelmed and flattered that it boosted my confidence and made me even more determined to excel in the world of dance. It was only in 1988 that dear Russell told me that the dance critic had been unavailable on the night of the performance and the paper's gardening critic had been roped in to write the review. The poor man was completely out of his depth so Russell had been forced to help out!

During the tour I met and married Terry James, a fellow dancer. I had received a persuasive offer from the Ballet de l'Opéra de Marseilles to return to France on a soloist contract. I replied with a telegram to the effect that if there was a place for my husband I would be available. The company accepted my proposal and we left New Zealand on the *Fairsky* in May 1964. The departure was less of a wrench than the first time. I was becoming an experienced traveller, and having a companion to share my joys and sorrows eased the farewells. I had found that attitudes had not changed in terms of the desirability and the prestige of working overseas. There was never any real question of my staying when I had been given the opportunity of more overseas experience.

We arrived in France in summer and lived in one room in a dingy *pension* opposite the stage door. We cooked on a small three-legged 'camp' gas burner balanced on the bidet. It was all very bohemian. I danced solo parts in major classical works and in contemporary ballets by the company's choreographer. We toured the Continent, danced at the Festivals of Spain and did a resident season in Marseilles in the winter, then packed for a holiday in London.

During our first week in London we attended a ballet class at the Dance Centre in Covent Garden. A sprightly, silver-grey-haired lady with twinkling eyes, and a handsome bearded man watched the class and afterwards asked if Terry and I would be interested in joining the new-look Ballet Rambert. We discovered that this elegant pair were the famed Dame Marie Rambert and Norman Morrice, who was later to become director of the Royal Ballet, Covent Garden. The well-known old classical company had been disbanded and, with the help of the Arts Council, a new company was to take its place under the 'all-seeing' eye of Mme Rambert, with Norman Morrice as artistic director. The new company was to consist of a nucleus of twelve dancers from the old company and a small number of dancers who had been with the Royal or Western Theatre Ballet. We were extremely lucky to be included. I spent five years with the New Ballet Rambert. These were exciting beyond belief. For the first six months we trained daily in both ballet and modern classes in the Martha Graham technique before embarking on rehearsals of the company repertoire.

Madame Rambert, affectionately known as 'Mim', watched every London performance. She shuffled dancers like cards, testing them in different roles until she discovered where their ability lay. She gave rousing speeches when necessary about breathing new life into dance in the United Kingdom. Her passion and commitment were infectious. We were introduced to a wide range of choreographers from MacMillan, Ashton and Tudor to Tetley, Sokolov, La Cotte, Van Danzig, Christopher Bruce and others. The guest teachers were some of the best in the world and Ballet Rambert continued to be the nurturing ground it had long been for aspiring young choreographers. We took part in workshops and collaborations with young designers and musicians. From Rambert emerged a long list of famous choreographers, teachers and performers.

The New Ballet Rambert rapidly developed a huge following, especially among the younger generation. We were making history as the first modern/contemporary dance company in Britain. To me it had a special character of its own. I felt totally enveloped, as if in an extended family where we shared both our domestic and professional interests. This camaraderie helped us survive the enormous mental and physical demands of constant performance.

I loved my time with New Ballet Rambert, where I danced almost all leading roles and learnt a great deal about dance and dancers. The Rambert years taught me the importance of nurturing and developing talent and the need for a balance between discipline and the freedom to develop personality in performance. The need for 'stage craft' and for dance performance to be articulate, calculated, well defined and at all times a well-packaged 'gift' for the audience to enjoy was impressed on us. As the company moved further into contemporary dance I longed for the exacting confines of classical dance and to put on my point shoes again.

My husband was at that time with the London Festival Ballet and the director, Beryl Grey, offered me a position in her company, but I had long been interested in joining the Western Theatre Ballet, with its steamy reputation for drama and fiery tempers. This company had an exciting repertoire and was resident at Sadlers Wells Theatre in London. In 1969 Peter Darrell, the much-loved artistic director of Western Theatre Ballet, offered me a position with the company. The day I joined them the British Arts Council, which controlled the funding, announced decentralisation plans and we were sent to Glasgow to become the Scottish Theatre Ballet! During the next seven years I danced all principal and minor roles, toured the world and met royalty. The company became internationally accepted. Darrell directed with great flair and it was love of him that kept most of us loyal to the company. We enjoyed a strong link with Denmark and the Bournonville style of dance. One of the highlights of dancing with the Scottish Theatre Ballet was working with Danish Bournonville specialist, Hans Brenna, who visited periodically as a guest teacher and producer. My greatest joy at this time was the arrival of my brother Christopher who subsequently settled in Britain. He writes and lectures in law at a London university.

The Scottish Ballet, sponsored by the British and Scottish Arts Council, pioneered dance in Scotland. Every year we toured Britain with seasons in London and at home; the company divided into two groups and performed in every nook and cranny with an acceptable hall or theatre. In 1975 I became a member of the first Scottish Advisory Council which took an active part in the development of future policy for the Scottish Ballet. Under Peter Darrell's guidance and the constant performance of leading roles, I developed rapidly in both technical and acting ability. I now had the maturity to recognise my strengths and brought these to bear in every role I danced. I enjoyed considerable success and critical acclaim as Giselle and La Sylphide, but the role which stands out in my memory was Mary Queen of Scots, for which I received a tremendous ovation on the opening night in London. I continually strove for that intangible magic that makes a performance memorable for the audience. During my time abroad I danced with many unforgettable male

117

partners, among them Rudolf Nureyev, Peter Schauffus, Anthony Dowell, Christopher Gable, David Holmes and Cristian Addams.

In 1973 I left a tour of *Giselle* in England to dance the title role in Auckland with the New Zealand Ballet. Jon Trimmer was Albrecht, Bryan Ashbridge played Hilarion. It had been nearly ten years since I had visited New Zealand. The prospect of returning home after so long was exciting, but it was overshadowed by anxiety. I was aware that I was being promoted as an internationally renowned principal dancer and I was anxious to live up to the expectations this created. As an expatriate New Zealander I felt enormous pressure and worried constantly about my ability to perform as well at home as I had abroad. I was vulnerable because being accepted in my own country meant so much to me. To appear before audiences who feel they know you personally is always a daunting prospect. My fears proved to be well founded. I had to battle against preconceived ideas and traditional attitudes to establish the role as I wished to perform it. My confidence was in danger of being eroded. I had developed an interpretation of the role of Giselle to appeal to contemporary audiences and was determined not to present Giselle as a museum piece. I had evolved a particular affinity for the part and hoped, as any performing artist should, that my interpretation would bring tears to as many eyes as possible. I knew I'd succeeded when, on opening night, after Giselle's death in Act 1, I lay on the stage floor and became aware of the sound of sobbing. I opened one eye to see the entire *corps de ballet* crying. I was elated. I had never been so happy to see people cry. To my mind the technical feats of the ballet, while needing to be as unblemished as possible, are secondary to the drama of the storyline. I felt great rapport in dancing with lovably eccentric Jon Trimmer, who was a caring partner in his moral and physical support. My determination to perform Giselle as I had been taught to interpret the role proved to be the right decision, for the season was a success. I was still under contract to the Scottish Ballet and had to leave for Scotland as soon as it was over. This time the parting from family and friends was not so traumatic as I was planning to return at the first opportunity.

The following year, 1974, Australian entrepreneur Michael Edgley arranged a tour of Australasia for the Scottish Ballet. We were joined by Margot Fonteyn and Ivan Nagy, who were great stars and great personalities. The pleasure of watching Margot, with her minute attention to detail, and to share with her the role of La Sylphide, was a great learning experience. She was a fun-loving, caring person. With husband Tito in his wheelchair in the wings, she gave magical performances. Ivan flew through the air as if suspended on wires, and the excitement of their partnership was tangible. When we arrived in Wellington the press reported that I received 'a heroine's welcome', but it was overshadowed by my overwhelming sadness that my father was lying critically ill in hospital in Palmerston North. Margot gave me tremendous support and sent my father her bouquets, and all the company mailed an individually signed card to wish him well. We pushed on to Dunedin, where the company was given a tremendous reception and piped across the tarmac by a pipe band with kilts flying. It was a welcome sight for the tired dancers after ten weeks of travelling and performing so far from their home base in Scotland. The tour ended in Dunedin, and when the company boarded the plane for England I rushed home to Palmerston North to be with my family. My father was able to come home from hospital, but, sadly, died two weeks later. Numbed, I had to leave for another tour, another contract.

My return to Scotland began one of the most exciting periods of my career. I was to be partnered by Rudoph Nureyev in several ballets. At the first rehearsal of the *pas de deux* in *Flower Festival at Genzano* he stated, 'You do what you do, I'll do what I do, and when we get together you do what I say.' It seemed fair comment to me. I was so in awe of him that I did exactly what I was told. Rudi worked extremely hard at all times and expected no less from his partner and those around him. I was sent to Brussels to rehearse with Maurice Béjart for his dramatic ballet, *Sonate à Trois*, based on the play *Huis Clos (No Exit)* by Jean-Paul Sartre. Jorge Donne, principal male dancer with the Béjart Ballet, rehearsed with me in Nureyev's place, as he was unavailable, in an amazingly large studio where the floor was wound up or lowered, depending on the level of the 'rake' one would be performing on next. When we finally played to the bejewelled audiences of Madrid, Robyn Haig and I danced this exhausting dramatic work with Nureyev. It was an experience not to be forgotten. The critic reported that I gave a magnificent performance. Little did he know that the drama I conveyed was enhanced by the diarrhoea and near pneumonia I was suffering. I felt as if I was dying but I wouldn't have missed those performances for the world. The time passed in a blur of standing ovations, excitement, total fatigue and complete elation. When we weren't performing, Rudi worked on, in woolly hat, as though his life depended on it. The rest of us could only attempt to follow his example.

In Paris I danced Queen of the Wilis to Lynn Seymour's Giselle and Rudi's Albrecht, at the huge, highly sprung Palais des Sports. It was like dancing on a trampoline which gave me the sensation of flying. At the Coliseum in London we danced *La Sylphide* for two weeks. There were some 3000 people in the audience for each performance. Half way through the second week Rudi finally gave in to damaged shins. Graham Bart replaced him and together we went on in fear and trepidation, expecting seats to bang as people left in disappointment. We made it through to the end with relief; never had two people concentrated so hard on the job in hand. There had been no audible departures or chanting of 'We want Rudi.' Back in the dressing room the door banged open and there stood Rudi. 'Well, Madame, I believe you were a success without me,' he smiled. Such praise could go to a girl's head!

My next major role was performing the title role in the ballet *Mary Queen of Scots* at Sadlers Wells. The ballet closed with Mary being beheaded. On opening night I stood for the first curtain call. I was elated by the overwhelming audience response and I automatically turned to see who they were applauding. I found I was alone. I could hardly believe that resounding applause was for me.

In 1976, after five years of procrastination, I married Englishman Michael Lloyd, who was then a conductor with the Scottish Ballet and is now associate artistic director of the English National Opera. Immediately after our marriage Michael joined a German opera company in Kassel. I stayed with the Scottish

Ballet, performing until I was five months pregnant and then joined him in Germany. Our son Nicholas was born in England and for the next few years we commuted between England and Germany as I continued to dance. We moved to Stuttgart and my mother arrived from New Zealand to become a very welcome and much valued babysitter when I travelled to perform in England and to work in Hong Kong.

I next returned to New Zealand in 1978 to take part in the *Sleeping Beauty* for the twenty-fifth anniversary celebrations of the New Zealand Ballet. We did innumerable performances and as a guest artist I performed every night. In Europe, principal dancers were expected to appear in a full-length ballet only every alternate night, and I found the New Zealand schedule exhausting. Here we were expected to maintain high standards night after night for weeks on end. My physique was not up to that sort of treatment and I became very run-down.

In 1979 I again returned, this time as stand-in artistic director to both stage and dance in *La Sylphide*, which I had lovingly directed in Hong Kong the year before. Over a period of several years I had received critical acclaim for dancing the title role and had been so looking forward to dancing this part in New Zealand. Unfortunately I tore a calf muscle after the first few performances and toured in plaster from ankle to knee. The plaster was removed as the tour drew to a close but I only managed to do a few more appearances. It was a great disappointment. On that tour was a frail-looking seventeen-year-old from Christchurch whom I could not take my eyes off, as I could see she was destined for the big time. Fiona Tonkin by name, she later became a principal dancer with the Australian Ballet. I would have liked to stay in New Zealand but my family were in Germany and I had work commitments, so I left for Europe after agreeing to return the following year to choreograph *The Nutcracker*.

When I came back I found that the company was still without a permanent director and was low on funds. We produced the ballet on a shoestring but, despite this, *The Nutcracker* was a box-office success and remained so for the next eleven years. I was gratified to see so much potential talent emerging from the New Zealand School of Dance, including Karin Wakefield and Martin

James who both went on to become principal dancers in New Zealand and abroad. I loved visiting home, but circumstances always took me away. Over the last few years my interests and experience had widened considerably to include teaching, choreography, production and direction. I believed I could offer new perspectives to the dance scene in New Zealand and desperately wanted to remain. The company was still without a director and although I was offered the position my age, personal situation and other commitments made acceptance impossible. I suggested an old colleague, Harry Haythorne, for the job, which he was subsequently offered and which he accepted. He became the artistic director and continued in the position until 1992.

Since 1978 I had enjoyed a continuing love affair with Hong Kong, where I went to teach, direct, choreograph and advise over a period of twelve years. It was humbling to be so revered and cherished by both the contemporary and classical dancers. Because of their trust and affection I gave without fear my best work, teaching from its inception the City Contemporary Dance Company. I developed repertoire and taught for the Hong Kong Ballet Group, Dance Federation, Academy of Performing Arts, and the Hong Kong Ballet. I was invited many times to stay as a director and teacher but felt if I was to move from my European base then New Zealand had to be my choice.

As one of the few western dancers ever to work in China, I was invited in 1987 to stage the first graduation performance of the Beijing Academy since the revolution. It was an honour to work with these amazing young dancers and fabulous teachers of pure classical style. They were wonderful people who showered me with kindness, which was all they had to give. Their commitment to dance was all the more admirable in light of the abject poverty in which they existed. If I could have lived two lives at once, I would have stayed. A couple of years later I happened to see one of those dancer/teachers from Beijing at a conference in Hong Kong. We did a little dance in the foyer of the hotel and embraced, then we did another little dance laughing all the while. We had no common language but we shared the joy and delight of happy memories and the pleasure of seeing each other again. We each knew exactly what the other was trying to say.

By 1983, when my daughter Katharine was born, I had a desperate yearning to return to New Zealand, but had accepted a contract with the British Ballet Theatre, which was formed in the 1980s to provide experience for young dancers with potential. British Ballet Theatre was a touring company which I joined for a ten-week tour to dance Giselle as a guest artist. Anton Dolin was the director of this traditional production and John Gilpin, despite his failing health, assisted with rehearsals. Both he and Dolin lived by the sarcastic quip, the gay banter of bitchery and gossip about other artists. They were great fun socially and usually attracted an audience. Dolin had always been kind about my performances since I had danced in his famous *Pas de Quatre* years earlier, and he likened me to prominent dancers of a past era. On one occasion he had brought Evelyn Laye, doyenne of the British stage, to see me after a performance. She stood in the doorway of my dressing room and with a velvety glove patted my hand, saying, 'My dear, you transported me, for which I thank you.' She must have been 70 years old, but was radiantly beautiful with the figure of a young girl and eyes that positively shone. She too had transported me many years earlier when I saw her perform at a theatre in the Strand.

In 1986 I was asked to be a guest artist again with the (now Royal) New Zealand Ballet, in Harry Haythorne's epic production of *Swan Lake*. It was an enjoyable experience, marred only by having to watch Sherilyn Kennedy battle against the odds to prove she was a noteworthy New Zealand dancer. I sympathised with her plight, remembering the pressures I also had experienced when I first returned to New Zealand and came under the spotlight.

It was at this time that I made the decision to return to live in New Zealand at the first opportunity. I had long yearned for my own patch of green and the comfort of the Ruahines and Tararuas which had been my solace in times of stress, but it was not until after teaching contracts with Expo in Vancouver, and the London Contemporary Dance School, plus a further trip to Hong Kong, that I once again came home. In 1987 I choreographed a ballet based on Katherine Mansfield's short story, *Bliss*. I was well aware that the dance industry in New Zealand was small and the types of positions for which I was qualified were few and far between. I mentioned to Anne Rowse, the director of the New Zealand School of Dance, my intention to return home permanently. Soon after I arrived back in Europe I was offered the position of tutor of classical ballet at the New Zealand School of Dance. I accepted with pleasure and began the awesome task of moving possessions and children half way across the world.

Coming home to the land of my birth and adjusting to life in New Zealand has at times been difficult, sometimes disappointing and lonely, but worth the effort to readjust. The complex process of moving, frustrating at times, brought back all the old fears and insecurities. I was afraid that I would not fit in, that I would have to fight against entrenched traditional attitudes and that the skills and experience I had to offer would not be easily accepted. It has taken me four years to settle down and get over the emotional upheaval of uprooting and transplanting to a way of life which was no longer familiar. When anyone innocently inquired as to how long I was staying, or when I was leaving, the old insecurities returned and I became anxious that I was not welcome. Comments such as, 'Why don't you go back, dear, there is nothing here for you', were hurtful. Nobody had said anything like that to me in any of the other countries where I had worked, and I found comments like this very difficult to cope with. During my travels I was continually a guest in other people's territories and I was always made welcome. I shared the lives of those with whom I worked and socialised and was always accepted for the skills and experience I had to offer. I expected the same from my countrymen and was sometimes disappointed. I found it hard to understand why some were unwilling to entertain new ideas which were already well accepted abroad. For a long time after returning I was confused and bewildered by changes I had not anticipated. The New Zealand intonation, the habit of understatement and the undemonstrative manner of the majority of New Zealanders made it difficult to gauge their feelings. Some of our European habits were hard to break. I found the children turning lights on all the time, a habit they had acquired living in London under grey skies where daylight disappears so much earlier. We discovered that we spoke more loudly than most people, the result of living in inner-city locations with high noise levels. I miss the frequent discussions about every aspect of theatre and dance, the exploration of new ideas and playing verbal tennis, without the discussion deteriorating into an argument. I had always had a great number of friends and found it hard to have to start making new ones all over again. Margot Fonteyn once remarked that I always seemed to have a family of people around me: I miss that. I believe it is easier to move to a new country than it is to return home, because home carries with it more personal expectations.

During my years as a performer I had always been interested in young dancers' problems and aspirations. I enjoyed helping them to develop technically and artistically and many of them now work in companies all over the word. Despite the fact that I had experience in teaching and coaching from beginners to principal dancers, I had never taught one group of people for more than three months at one time. I was unprepared for the fact that it is quite different teaching the same people over a three-year period. I find it takes all my knowledge, experience, optimism and patience to provide the students with the learning environment and care they so need.

Timing is very important. The performer in me knows this. Adjusting to the pace and rhythm of life in New Zealand has taken longer than I expected. I will always be grateful and in debt to the few who have helped me make that transition, who accepted me and were there through the difficult times. Having spent twenty-six years away from New Zealand I find I am often considered an outsider, yet I have always been fiercely proud of being a New Zealander. Having worked and lived in the theatre capitals of the world it is easy to see the New Zealand dance industry in relation to the outside world, identify the needs, and map a path which would further its development. I have discovered that change cannot be hurried, but I hope to be able to use my hard-earned skills to further the development of dancers in New Zealand. I continue to get requests to work abroad, but for now my commitment is here with 'my hills'. Coming home has given me peace of mind. The circle is complete.

# Suspensions and Resolutions:
## Words About Music

## John Mansfield Thomson

I grew up in one of the remoter parts of New Zealand, in the small town of Blenheim, capital of the province of Marlborough, with a population of around 6,000. The tawny tussock-clad Wither Hills formed part of our playground, especially the old brick factory at their feet, where, with a group of local children, we raced perilously downhill on the remnants of the trolleys that had survived, and talked endlessly with each other about everything under the sun. Ten miles away at Rarangi, 'Cloudy Bay', the steep shingly beach hissed and roared, my grandfather's stately blue Hudson would become stuck in the stones and we would gather manuka branches to help ease it out. A steep path led to nearby Monkey Bay where the waves plucked at the swirling fronds of kelp and from an underground cavern issued eerie noises and sometimes veils of spray as the seas rolled in and out.

The port of Picton at the head of Queen Charlotte Sound lay twenty miles to the north, with a road which wound ribbon-like beside what was known as the 'Swamp', a tangle of flaxes, submerged trees and reeds, an untidy sight then, but now an ecological treasure. In Picton we spent most of our holidays, with long summer days rowing, fishing, picnicking on the harbour, my two sisters, my cousins, our friends and I entirely on our own and trusted, even without lifejackets, to be sensible about boats and the sea. Each one of us could swim and we respected the prohibitions placed upon us not to leave the confines of the harbour, not to turn beam on to a southerly, and many similar matters. Back in Blenheim itself, we swam in nearby streams and small rivers, taking for granted a climate described, along with Nelson, as the finest in New Zealand. Unbeknown to us then and unappreciated until much later, those bright clear days and sharp frosty winters made it, in the words of a visiting friend from England, like 'some Garden of Eden'.

But all Edens must be left, journeyed from, and sometimes returned to, and my travels took me three times to London and England and back. The third of these, the temporary visit that should have been six months, but which instead stretched over twenty years from 1961 to 1983, proved the most important. Nearly all Edens also have their serpents and ours took the form of a cruel regime wreaked upon my two sisters and me by a Scottish orphan maid who lived in at my grandmother's and whose sadistic impulses took the form of destroying books, school readers, billiard tables and cues, top hats and watches, to say nothing of myriad other mishaps such as galoshes being found in my grandmother's flour bin. But this, as I have said elsewhere, is another story, and one worthy of a Henry James. I mention it here to offset any impression that ours was some charmed, idyllic life. Few childhoods are, and this was no exception, being marred in a fundamental sense by the long and courageously sustained illness of my mother, who contracted tuberculosis when I was five and died when I had just turned twelve, followed by the deaths of my father when I was sixteen and my grandmother, who looked after us, the following year.

We had been brought up in a musical household where my mother, Frances Jean Wemyss, sang and played the piano. My father could manage piano duets with her, and my uncles sang ballads on Sunday evenings, dapper Uncle Cyril being in demand on social occasions and as soloist in the annual *Messiah*. My cousin, Elizabeth Wemyss, a year older than I, already had the makings of an accomplished pianist, which she became, before launching out in a pioneer role as an excellent choral conductor, founder of the St Andrew's Singers of Blenheim in the

1960s and the Elizabeth Wemyss Singers in Christchurch a decade later. Far grander than any of us was my paternal grandmother's cousin, Rosina Buckman, who was talked about constantly, but like children everywhere we never quite believed what our elders told us. Had she really sung at Covent Garden, been Sir Thomas Beecham's principal dramatic soprano, a great Isolde and one of New Zealand's most distinguished singers?

From the age of five we learned the piano at the local convent from kind Sister de Pazzi and her real sister, crosspatch Sister Augustine, who rapped our fingers with a ruler, and inflicted penance by ordering extra practice on Saturday mornings in the chapel while she scrubbed the steps outside, interrupting her work from time to time to shout, 'Wrong note!' In Sister de Pazzi's more friendly room we jumped up and down to learn the different time signatures and copied out scales in boredom and bewilderment at tables on the wooden verandah.

My father always seemed of a more literary and entrepreneurial than musical disposition, for he wrote well, had been a skilled journalist in his first job on the *Marlborough Express*, until he left for the First World War, and had once been offered the position of manager of the Wellington Opera House. He became, however, the agent for visiting artists, and I would often see a singer or a pianist in his book and music shop, bent gloomily over the conspicuously few crosses on the box plan of the vast His Majesty's Theatre, in which we almost invariably felt ashamed of our home town for its thin straggle of an audience.

I first arrived in England in April 1945, shortly before VE Day and the end of the Second World War, and soon after the last V2 had dropped on two blocks of flats in Whitechapel and demolished them. As a third-class naval airman in the Fleet Air Arm, I had been posted overseas for training after three weeks' naval initiation at HMNZS *Tamaki* in Auckland Harbour, where we learned to tie knots, sleep in a hammock, pull a cutter (not 'row' as another naval friend scornfully pointed out) and do other similarly nautical things. I used to feel the Navy took all the fun and romance out of the sea as that sense of awe, respect and love that had developed over the years, latterly through sailing small boats in the Sounds, was subjugated to Manuals of Instruction. After *Tamaki* and 'final leave' we waited impatiently in barracks for a ship, until one Sunday afternoon this artificial life ended. Threading our way through a harbour shimmering with yachts and small craft, we set out on the old *Ruahine* for Panama, New York and England.

My uncle had sailed on her to Britain in the First World War, and at the outbreak of hostilities in 1939 she had been rescued from a ship's graveyard in the Clyde and returned to service. The *Ruahine*'s stern quarters reserved for servicemen seemed unbelievably austere, even compared to the Union Steam Ship Company's Picton ferry, the *Tamahine* with its starched linen tablecloths and silverware. Fancy travelling to England on such a dowdy ship. Nevertheless, she rode out an Atlantic March hurricane with supreme assurance, giving us the sensation below decks of being in an old, creaky but comfortable wicker basket. A little later on that same voyage from New York she nearly ended her days when our convoy was attacked by a U-boat on a pristine spring morning off the coast of Spain. Germany had by now clearly lost the war but as a participant at the time in naval patrols wrote: 'there was no noticeable diminution in the destructive fervour of the U-boat Arm'. With the aid of a newly developed telescopic periscope which allowed it to penetrate into our midst, the submarine sent two torpedoes across our bows to explode on the waterline in the hull of a large tanker beside us. Within minutes it had turned into a flaming inferno which gradually settled further and further down into the water. From our decks we watched numbed as the crew ran desperately from side to side until we were marshalled in lifejackets on the other deck, ready to abandon ship if necessary, as depth charges exploded all around us and planes from the pocket aircraft carriers flew low in their hunt for the killer. Were the torpedoes intended for us, for the commodore's ship nearby or for the tanker? It was an unanswerable question, but most probably they were indeed meant for the tanker, from which not a single soul was saved.

The convoy had already fanned out and scattered: re-routed to Tilbury instead of Liverpool, our original destination, we entered the fantasy-like landscape of the Thames Estuary, suffused by a pale misty sunlight, on our own. On each side of the river lay the wrecks of bombed and mined ships and every now and again appeared a moon-walk kind of structure, a steel fortress whose legs straddled the mud and the water. From across the channel came the muffled sound of explosions. At Tilbury we boarded a train for Waterloo Station. I could not believe my first sight of the city – the endless rows of grimy, ugly and destitute-looking houses, the marks on every hand of savage assault from the air, and the general dirt, neglect and feeling of exhaustion. We waited restlessly on Waterloo Station, sampling weak English mild and bitter, until in the early hours of the morning we headed for Portsmouth in Hampshire and our destination, the Fleet Air Arm station at Lee-on-Solent.

I was just nineteen and, improbably, had been flight sergeant of our local unit of the Air Training Corps in Blenheim, where my elementary knowledge of navigation and morse helped lead me at eighteen to join the Fleet Air Arm. With its combination of air and sea, elements I had grown up with, it also provided the swiftest possible escape from the life of a clerk in my uncle's Bank of New Zealand.

Early next morning on a sparkling spring day we changed trains at a small local station in the countryside. Along the platform lay the London papers, stacked up in deep piles, from the *Times* and the *Daily Telegraph*, to the *News Chronicle, Daily Express, Daily Mail* and *Mirror*. British forces had just entered the German concentration camp of Belsen and we walked past pictures of wagons piled high with emaciated corpses, of living skeletons hovering between life and death. These revelations swept like some shockwave over Britain and the civilised world.

I took my demobilisation in Britain in early 1946, a passion for the theatre having led me to walk into the headquarters of ENSA (Entertainment National Services Association) at Drury Lane Theatre while on leave in London and ask if they had a vacancy for an assistant stage manager. Eventually I joined one of their companies touring the mining districts of South Wales, including Aberfan, Merthyr Tydfil and the Rhondda Valley, a grim environment in which we encountered much warmth and friendliness. We presented but one play, the comedy *See How They Run* by Philip King, which seemed far too insubstantial for our realist audiences. Afterwards I returned to London and sought training in the theatre. As no courses for producers or directors then existed, I enrolled for the third term of the first year of the general acting course of the Central School of Art and Drama at the Albert Hall, where Claire Bloom, later the star of Charles Chaplin's film *Limelight*, stood out as an exceptional talent.

However, I learned most not from the Central School but from attending morning orchestral rehearsals in the Albert Hall, thus having a preview of the evening's concert. Day after day I sat upstairs in the balcony close to the conductor so I could hear his remarks, sometimes quite withering and often witty, as with Sir Thomas Beecham, but almost always illuminating. Sir Adrian Boult, Sir Malcolm Sargent, John Barbirolli, George Weldon and Basil Cameron were among those leading English wartime conductors who conducted there regularly, with brilliant European visitors such as Victor de Sabata in electrifying Beethoven and the Verdi *Requiem*.

At the end of this first year I did not return to the School but had to find work, so became a temporary copy typist for an agency which assigned me to an architectural firm and to an export company where I typed invoices for hairpins for India while that continent underwent the paroxysms of riots, a prelude to partition the following year. I bought a bicycle and took it on trains into the countryside and cycled extensively. Although I tried to like England as warmly as did some of my fellow New Zealanders who had also taken demobilisation there, some hesitation held me back. I missed the openness and spontaneity of life in New Zealand, the freedom of the Sounds, the clean air and sun. The first washing I hung on the line in Camden Town had to be redone, it had become so grimy. And I deeply disliked all the manifestations of class.

At this point I obtained a £10-a-week position as assistant stage manager with a new small repertory company in the Playhouse at Broadstairs, a characterful seaside resort about ninety minutes by train from London, notable for its associations with

Dickens and later with Edward Heath. I learned the basics of stage lighting and how to work a switchboard, elementary as ours was, borrowed period furniture from the local antique shops, acted small parts such as the Welsh boy in Emlyn Williams' *The Corn Is Green*, and took the juvenile lead in *The Ghost Train*.

Alas, our new repertory company began its life towards the end of summer and audiences fell off with the approach of winter. One morning we were all summoned on stage to be addressed by our businessman backer from the industrial north and the father of our lead actor and director, to be thanked for our valiant efforts to bring in audiences and to be told our salaries had henceforth to be reduced to ten shillings a week. At this point I decided my short theatrical career had come naturally to an end. I wrote to Victoria University College in Wellington to inquire about completing my BA degree, my studies having begun on the deck of the *Ruahine*, thanks to an enlightened Forces education officer who signed me up for stage I English, which I had sat and passed in the sepulchral examination halls of South Kensington.

Back in New Zealand as a student at Victoria the memories of that year in Britain haunted me. Its innumerable legacies ranged from the joy of hearing Shakespeare and the English language spoken with such rhythmic vitality, to a sense of the qualities of good arts criticism as practised in the daily papers. I had also acquired a new interest in architecture. But I felt I had still scarcely penetrated the fabric of English life and understood little of how its society worked. I knew that one day soon I must return.

The second London visit took place in 1949, less than three years later. The compulsory Anglo-Saxon and Middle English papers of the BA had been a torture in no circumstances to be repeated. Should I wait another full year in order to do history III followed by history honours? I decided not. This time I worked my way to England as a greaser in the engine room on another New Zealand Company ship, the *Rakaia*, although I had really hoped to be taken on as a waiter. Covered with grime and oil I might be seen tipping waste over the stern by my fellow countrymen on the upper deck, amongst whom was my former lecturer in Middle English, Bob Burchfield, then a Rhodes Scholar, and an old friend, Bernard Knowles, on his way to take up an accountancy scholarship.

In London, I eventually enrolled for the postgraduate diploma in social anthropology at University College, a two-year course under Professor Daryll Forde, an authority on Africa. At the same time I studied typography at Camberwell School of Arts, gaining an invaluable overall view of printing processes, supplemented by the designing of advertisements, posters and concert programmes, including one for my cousin Elizabeth Wemyss's first piano recital in London, all of these now looking very much products of their time.

I did not complete the anthropology course, having gradually lost interest in what turned out to be a severely academic regime: English anthropology was then far behind American, both conceptually and in the structure of its training. Our sense of frustration may be illustrated by recalling the words of a fellow student who unfolded an elaborate kinship system table from a textbook with the comment: 'They're not happy until they've reduced everybody to this.' A slight exaggeration, perhaps, but more than a little right in spirit.


My third expedition to London in 1961 began as a short refresher course in contemporary music. I was at that time working in Sydney on a biography of the composer, Alfred Hill. Originally supported by a Literary Fund grant of £300, work was sustained by a position with the Australasian Performing Right Association in Sydney. Just before his ninetieth birthday in November 1960, Alfred Hill had died. By now, like many biographers, I felt ill at ease with my choice of subject, caused partly by my realisation of the lack of development and conservatism of much of Alfred's musical style and partly by the difficulties inherent in portraying a life that had become quite static by the 1930s, when Alfred was in his sixties.

When I first arrived in Australia in the late 1950s, the Sydney Symphony had recently lost its gifted conductor, Sir Eugene Goossens, arrested at Sydney airport for presumably bringing pornographic literature into the country. David Marr's recent brilliant biography of Patrick White gives an added sense of how such an action typified the puritanical, vengeful and self-righteous mores of the period. Australian musical life thereafter became increasingly less vital. Although Richard Meale's Sonata for Flute, which premiered (to the horror of many in the audience) at the Sydney Conservatorium, heralded the new wave of Australian composers who were to include Sculthorpe, Butterley and others, none of them was yet active. Richard Meale fought a lone battle against the musical establishment. My absorption of the German avant-garde periodical *Die Reihe*, lent to me by an Australian composer friend, John Antill, whose ballet score *Corroboree* had been discovered by Goossens, confirmed my sense of being trapped in some kind of musical aspic.

New Zealand, by comparison, had been forward-looking, with the YC radio programmes that included the contemporary music series of the American Louisville Orchestra, Frederick Page's broadcasts of Boulez, Berio and Stockhausen, Lilburn premieres, and an active International Society for Contemporary Music. John Antill asked why I wanted to return to Europe and I told him it was my last chance to catch up. Moreover, I could never satisfactorily complete the Hill book while living in Sydney. I booked a passage on the *Fairsky*, a converted pocket aircraft carrier and one of the numerous ships then engaged in ferrying new Australians from Europe and taking tourists back at cheap rates. I told my Sydney friends and especially Alfred Hill's widow, Mirrie, that I would be back in six months. Australia had proved a more than stimulating experience. I had eagerly absorbed its literature, art, architecture and history, for instance, and had appreciated the openness, warmth, gusto and positive qualities of the Australian. I fully expected to return.

Fate, destiny, accident or design decreed otherwise. After visiting New York to help Barbara McKenzie and her husband, Findlay, who were preparing a book on Australian singers, I spent three astonishing months as an observer at Friedelind

Wagner's Bayreuth Masterclass of 1962. Back in London, after a talk on the role of the Australian composer to the Composers' Guild of Great Britain, Richard Arnell asked if I would help him launch a new publication to supersede their cyclostyled journal called the *Composer*. The tribulations of the first issue are a tale in themselves: the designer/publisher went bankrupt and the bailiffs actually moved in, the first time I had seen them carry off a table and a carpet. The printer held on to the type awaiting payment and the first issue was rushed through with such haste that it emerged looking like a typographer's nightmare. But the Composers' Guild were generous and invited me to continue. I secured a gifted designer in Craig Dodd (now also an authority on ballet), and we went to the Shenval Press, then one of Britain's leading design printing houses. The second issue with its elegant blue cover set new standards in British musical publications. The third number captured wide attention through its topical articles – Wilfrid Mellers on the American scene, two teenage girls on the Beatles, and especially Peter Racine Fricker's 'The Vanishing Composers', an analysis of the British content in current orchestral programming which elicited spirited (and at times indignant) comment in the national press. My original contact with the *Composer* had been from Sydney, when I sent an article to its editor, Stephen Dodgson. The publisher Barrie & Rockliff later invited Stephen to be their music books editor, but he demurred and instead put forward my name.

Armed with the handsome second issue of *Composer*, I gained the position, although its actual duties (and remuneration) seemed somewhat vague. Barrie & Rockliff ranked amongst London's leading publishers of music books. Their offices lay beside the law courts in a Victorian building served by a water lift under the aegis of the Thames Water Company. In winter the liftman tended the bright coke fire in my room. Donald Mitchell, then music books editor for Faber and at work on the second volume of his Mahler epic, was to be the first Barrie author I met, and thus began what became a long friendship.

I had never edited a *book* before in my life, let alone one on music, with all its complexities of music examples and the engagement of copyists. It was my task to reanimate the Barrie list, to 'tend the garden' as Leopold Ullstein, the German-born director, put it, and restore it to its former place. This proved difficult for somebody who had only recently arrived and whose musical contacts lay principally with the Composers' Guild. The first manuscript I accepted and edited entirely on my own initiative was Philip Barford's *The Keyboard Music of Carl Philipp Emanuel Bach* – a baptism of fire, for it drew a very long hostile review from Stanley Sadie in the *Musical Times* ('This is an important but deeply flawed book . . .'). Otherwise it had excellent notices and held the field for many years after.

Music books gradually gathered a momentum which made my department as prolific as any. Major titles included Wilfrid Mellers' brilliant *Music in a New Found Land*, on American music; Alan Walker's *Chopin Companion*; Carl Flesch's monumental *Violin Fingering*; and several fine Hungarian books, notably Bence Szabolcsi's profound *The History of Melody*. Music book publishing is a specialised area where one must tread cautiously and with sure knowledge. Only 1200 to 2000 copies of each title were usually printed for Britain and the Commonwealth – an American sale could make a world of difference. With Alan Walker's *Chopin Companion* I had suggested a print run of 2500 and a lower price of fifty shillings, expecting proportionately larger sales, but these never eventuated. It proved a small specialised market.

Around the mid-1960s the pattern of English publishing began to change. Smaller, often distinguished and more traditional houses found themselves vulnerable to takeovers by bigger and usually international combines. Barrie & Rockliff had subsumed Herbert Jenkins, the small firm whose reputation was built largely on P.G. Wodehouse and a successful fresh-water fishing list, with some good music books such as the English Church Music series. Accompanying these changes was the virtual extinction of what in the trade is known as a backlist, when publishers carried stocks for many years of books they believed to be important. Remaindering had been quite uncommon. However, when Barrie & Rockliff were themselves taken over by a multinational and there began the reign of the accountants and marketing managers, who appraised the value of titles by their position on the sales charts, I saw almost every music book I had edited, including Norman Del Mar's classic three-volume *Richard Strauss*, abandoned to the discount shops. Very soon it had to be reprinted.

I was now deeply involved in *Composer*, which was gradually establishing itself, and with the music list of Barrie & Jenkins, as it had become. At this time two tempting possibilities came from the other side of the world, a critic's position on the *Sydney Morning Herald* and correspondence with Charles Brasch over the possibility of the future editorship of *Landfall*. Having considered these options most carefully, I concluded that were I to leave London at this point I should have achieved little, for publishing is like planting a forest which needs time to reach maturity. I stayed in London, not in any spirit of rejection of either Australia or New Zealand, but with a desire and need to bring to fruition the projects which I had started. I think one rarely 'decides' to become an expatriate, the choice is far too complex for that. So I became an editor of music books and journals, and before long added the *Recorder Magazine*, published by Schott, to the list. This stemmed from an interest in the instrument which had begun when the poet Pat Wilson presented me with a wooden descant and an instruction book. Later, I turned to the flute.

After several productive years at Barrie's, Alan Frank invited me to join Oxford as music books editor, and at the same time a similar invitation came from Donald Mitchell at Faber. Britain's newest music publishing company, Faber Music, had just been launched, based then on a single composer, Benjamin Britten, who had recently left Boosey & Hawkes following a dispute. As director, Donald found the music side occupied more and more of his time and he could no longer manage the Faber books.

I decided to join Donald and his assistant, Martin Kingsbury, and shared a tiny crowded office with them, amazingly never once getting in each other's way. Next door were the secretary, the production manager, the New Zealander Roderick Biss, and other Faber staff, including a young lady who each day despatched downstairs a massive wicker trolley packed full of rejected poetry books.

Working at Faber was in many ways like returning home, for I had grown up with so many of their authors, such as Siegfried Sassoon, and once I went down to the basement to gaze in awe at the shelves of numbered files marked 'TSE' (T.S. Eliot), raw material for the publication of his letters, then in progress. When I left Faber in the early 1970s my career as music books editor came to an end: I felt I had given to it and learned from it as much as I could. I had made many lasting friendships amongst my authors, and edited some notable books, such as James Blades' *Percussion Instruments and Their History*, the *Monteverdi* and *Beethoven Companions*, and the Stravinsky/Craft *Dialogues and a Diary*. Now I turned to a new project, the launching of a quarterly to be called *Early Music*.

I had tried to interest Schott in this venture and widen the appeal of what had become *Recorder and Music* to include all early instruments, notably lute, viol and harpsichord. At first, agreement seemed likely, but partly because of pressure from the German side of Schott in Mainz and from within the British recorder movement, ten days before the first issue went to press the managing director of Schott summoned me and asked me to abandon the venture and continue as before. With the beginnings of the first issue of an early music journal on my hands, I cast around for a publisher: Macmillan and Oxford seemed the most promising. I telephoned Alan Frank at Oxford, whom I already knew, and put the idea to him. Six months later, as he climbed out of his car at the *Notes and Embellishments* exhibition at Yoxford, near Aldeburgh, he remarked, 'I've got the green light from the delegates.' He wanted the first issue of *Early Music* to appear in January 1973 to coincide with their celebration of fifty years of music publishing.

A new era began which propelled me into the musical life of Europe, America and the rest of the world. With great flair Alan Frank asked Roger Davies, then a principal Oxford designer, to work with us: in his initial sketches Roger produced an innovatory and most imaginative plan which became the basis of the journal's visual distinction. Advertising fell under the entrepreneurial genius of Arthur Boyars, poet *manqué* and not so *manqué*, for he later translated Yevtushenko and toured in poetry readings with him, hurling wine glasses to the floor in Slavic abandon. During those first ten years *Early Music* established itself as the international voice of nearly every aspect of a movement which had revolutionised our approach to the study and performance of the music of the past. This history has, on my side, yet to be written.

Although *Early Music* proved the most challenging thing I had ever done, and seemed to expand in ever-widening circles embracing all of music, I still could not quell an inner voice which said, 'You should be back working in New Zealand.' My first return visit for six weeks in 1973-74 had proved a revelation. In March that year, just after the first issue of the new journal, I had been stricken by a coronary, most inconveniently in Balls Brothers Wine Bar in The Strand during lunch with Alec Hyatt King, then Keeper of Music at the British Library. We afterwards intended to walk across Waterloo Bridge to see *Notes and Embellishments*, on exhibition at the Royal Festival Hall. An ambulance strike left me dependent on a taxi to reach hospital, but a series of ancillary strikes in the outpatient departments meant that those nearest were closed and we were waved on by the pickets. By now considerable time had elapsed and I was in grave danger. By good fortune I managed to locate a German friend across the Heath who rang her own doctor, sped over in her car and took me to the only hospital open in the area, New End. As we drove past Golders Hill Park I felt certain that I was dying, as indeed I was, but not liking to frighten her I gazed instead at what I thought might be the last bright blue crocuses that I would ever see, springing up under the trees. In these circumstances, and following my recovery, a generous friend who would probably still wish to remain anonymous sent me the £300 airfare to New Zealand, and in December 1973 I returned for the first time for twelve years.

The visit had an extraordinary effect. I had forgotten the clarity and brilliance of light, the strength and power of the landscape: I was flooded with childhood impressions and dazed by the warmth of memory kindled by family and old and new friends. I travelled part of the time with an elderly Romanian-born friend, Alex Eldon, who on his first visit to London as a young man just after the First World War had heard Rosina Buckman sing Isolde at Covent Garden. When we reached Queenstown, with the sunset flooding the Remarkables in a wash of rapidly changing colours, he stood on the hotel balcony, flung wide his arms and declared: 'Claridges and the Savoy, they're finished, finished!'

On my return to London in February 1974 I stepped at once into the drear circumstances of the Heath government's stance against the miners. Coal supplies were dwindling. Oxford University Press in Conduit Street was lit by candles several days a week. The telephonist was wrapped up in a winter coat, as were the staff upstairs. Outside on the street a generator pounded away providing power to those offices which had organised their own system. The contrast with the summer in New Zealand could not have been more dramatic.

I became haunted by the vision of the New Zealand landscape I had experienced and could not put it out of my thoughts and senses. Summers in London became a particular torment, despite the success of *Early Music* and the constant arrival of American and Continental musicians and friends. I felt encapsulated and separated from a youthful heritage and a culture which had once been my own. Three years passed as *Early Music* prospered and became ever more demanding, but the bright glow engendered by that visit had not dimmed.

My eventual return came about through a project for a book. I had always wished to write a history of music in New Zealand and felt that this is what the original Hill biography should probably have been. Having prepared the somewhat telegraphic New Zealand entry for the *New Grove Dictionary of Music and Musicians* in the early seventies, this project now took on an insistent nature. Its realisation came about in a convoluted way. Around 1975 Roderick Biss, who had now re-settled in New Zealand as a partner in Price Milburn Music but operated from Auckland, put forward an idea for a symposium on Douglas Lilburn, to which I agreed to contribute if it found a publisher. Douglas, however, turned the project down, feeling it inappropriate to single out one particular composer at that time. Other similar approaches met with the same response. From his remote

Central Otago farmhouse Douglas then evolved an entirely separate visionary scheme for a project covering the whole spectrum
of music in New Zealand. After many vicissitudes a commission
for the book was proposed by the QEII Arts Council in association with the Australasian Performing Right Association (later
the Composers Foundation).

In December 1976 I once more set off for New Zealand, this
time to write the book whose scope was guided by Douglas's
original synopsis. Dan Davin had been instrumental in getting
the project through the delegates of Oxford University Press and
the original length of 100,000 words, agreed on then, was never
again revised. The nature of the book was also never re-formu-
lated, which eventually proved a source of extreme difficulty for
me. I felt virtually torn to pieces by the competing expectations
as to what the book ought to be. It is a fiction that in such circumstances an author is free to write what he wishes.

This visit could not be the same as that of 1973-74: nature and
human psychology demonstrated their fickleness. Whereas before, without effort, doors had opened to childhood and youthful perceptions, this time they tended to remain obstinately
closed, although the landscape still cast its intense spell with
almost supernatural moments, as after a visit to Douglas in his
Central Otago farm when we motored away across a luminous,
once-glacial scene that resembled a Wagner stage set. I soon
realised that the task was more demanding than I had imagined,
even with the experience of working on the Hill material. New
Zealand had been musically alive and alert almost since the first
decade of settlement, to say nothing of the vigorous Maori musical culture that had preceded it. Research into New Zealand
musical history had still scarcely begun.

Somehow these expeditions were fitted into the continuing
editorship of *Early Music*, though not without extended work-
loads on both sides of the globe. I think that this was an aspect
of the project that many in New Zealand never fully realised:
that I continued to edit *Early Music* while pursuing the New
Zealand research. The loyalty of my London staff proved exemplary and inspiring, led by Mrs Margot Leigh Milner: they dedicated themselves to keeping the journal going and to helping

141

me. This pattern continued until 1982 when my medical condition deteriorated and chronic angina (which revealed itself soon after my return from New Zealand in 1978) worsened. After near extinction in an ill-advised drug trial at the Royal Free Hospital in Hampstead, I underwent bypass heart surgery in Dunedin under Professor Pat Molloy, who had also operated successfully on my sister Shirley for the same condition.

This dramatically changed the tenor of my life. But at the same time grave problems developed with Oxford University Press, due largely to the crassness of a particular executive who exerted control over us from the Journals Department. His insensitivity to the issues involved proved to be the factor that tipped the scales. In summary, I think I felt that such a book as a history could not be satisfactorily written from the outside on the basis of short visits, however intensive they had been. I resigned from *Early Music* and handed over to Nicholas Kenyon, then recently returned from several years as music critic on the *New Yorker*, where he had gained a high reputation. Nicholas edited *Early Music* with aplomb for almost as long as I did, resigning in early 1992 to become Controller of Music on BBC Radio 3.

At first New Zealand seemed like a foreign country. I had grown away from its wellsprings of behaviour and forgotten about its chronic exasperations coupled with its resentments towards those who had lived and worked overseas. But walking amidst the Wellington landscape, for instance, with its distant skyline of hills, seascapes and colours, remained a continual stimulus. I tried to catch up on all the new developments in history, archaeology, natural resources, literature, painting, politics and music since my departure. I started work on a commissioned history of the Music Federation, completed a small book of musical caricatures and returned to the big History. Working with Janet Paul on Frederick Page's journal proved a specially rewarding task, despite the hazards of finding a publisher.

I had returned to a very different New Zealand, one in which the women's movement, for instance, seemed stronger and more vocal than in Britain, and the abundant graffiti, such as that emblazoned everywhere – 'The Treaty is a fraud' – at first puzzled me. What a simplistic view of New Zealand history we had imbibed at school. It took time to realise the full extent of the racial problems which all of European descent had inherited, however unwittingly. Soon the Waitangi Tribunal and the many books on the Treaty were to set out an imperative new task, as a whole range of historical truths revealed the magnitude of so many past injustices against the Maori people. If New Zealand was to become a truly moral society, these legacies of a continuous and seemingly hidebound deviousness had to be identified and resolved.

In this critical process of adjustment and change, when the older, more charitable and kinder New Zealand is being whittled away, music and all the arts have a fundamental role to play. Guardians and exemplars of a whole range of spiritual verities and diversities, whether European, Polynesian, Asian or African, they bind together a culture, permeate and enrich it, but most importantly they can also transform it.

# Notes on Contributors

*Sunny Amey* has had a lifelong interest in education as well as drama, and has always been interested in the educative possibilities of drama. Winning a New Zealand Government bursary allowed her to study with the English Stage Company at the Royal Court Theatre in London. Subsequently she had many theatre production jobs in England, including at the National Theatre with Sir Laurence Olivier. She returned to New Zealand to direct Downstage Theatre, Wellington, from 1970-74, and subsequently worked with the Education Department to develop drama in schools. She was director at the New Zealand Drama School from 1989-91.

*Sharon Crosbie* OBE was educated at Victoria and Harvard Universities. She has been a print journalist and worked with talk-back radio, but is best known for her National Radio *Nine to Noon* programme. She is Chairman of the Board of the National Drama School, and was recently appointed by Simon Upton to chair the National Advisory Committee on Core Health Services.

*Christopher Doig* OBE won the Mobil Song Quest in 1972 and studied singing at the Vienna Academy from 1974-76. He was a soloist tenor with the Vienna State Opera, 1976-80, and principal tenor with the Linz Opera, 1980-84. Additionally he sang at the Salzburg Festival, and at La Scala and other opera houses. He returned to New Zealand as director of the Christchurch Arts Centre, 1984-88, and assisted in founding the Canterbury Opera Company. From 1988-92 he was Wellington-based as director of the New Zealand Festival of the Arts. He is now Christchurch-based and pursues his international opera career from there.

*John Drawbridge*, painter and printmaker, studied at Wellington Teachers' Training College before winning the National Art Gallery Travelling Scholarship which enabled him to study for three years at the Central School of Art and Craft in London. A fourth year extension of the scholarship enabled him to study in Paris. While working in London several exhibitions of his works were shown, and he was commissioned to paint a mural in the reception hall of the new New Zealand House in the Haymarket. Subsequently he was commissioned to do a mural for the New Zealand Pavilion at Expo in Osaka in 1970 (a work later installed in the entrance foyer of the National Library in Wellington), and for the banquet hall of the Beehive. One of his more recent public works is stained glass windows in the chapel of the Home of Compassion, Island Bay.

*The Reverend Rodney Macann* has sung most major bass-baritone roles in opera houses round the world, as well as concerts in Carnegie Hall, New York, the Albert Hall, London, and the Philharmonic Hall, Berlin. He was a member of the English National Opera, 1985-90, and made many guest appearances at Covent Garden. Major performances have also occurred in Israel, the Soviet Union, France, Italy, Greece, Japan and Australia. Currently he is minister at the Central Baptist Church, Wellington, but he continues to be in demand to sing internationally.

*Dame Malvina Major* studied singing with Dame Sister Mary Leo. She won the Mobil Song Quest in 1963 and the Melbourne Sun Aria Contest in 1964. She trained at the London Opera Centre, 1965-67, and won the Kathleen Ferrier Scholarship in 1966. Since then she has sung to great acclaim at the Salzburg Festival, and in many opera houses and concert halls all over the world. Although she maintains her New Zealand home, she is constantly in demand overseas.

*Robin Morrison* is a free-lance photographer specialising in portrait photography and photo-journalism. His first major book, *The South Island of New Zealand: From the Road,* won the New Zealand Book Award for non-fiction in 1982. His most recent book, *At Home and Abroad,* won the New Zealand Book Award for book production in 1992. Several other books include a collaboration with Keri Hulme, *Homeplaces,* in 1989.

*Richard Mulgan* has written several books which include *Aristotle's Political Theory, Democracy and Power in New Zealand,* and *Maori, Pakeha and Democracy*. He was Professor of Classics and then of Politics at the University of Otago, 1970-89, and is currently Professor of Political Studies at the University of Auckland.

*The Most Reverend Sir Paul Reeves* studied at Victoria University of Wellington, St John's Theological Seminary, Auckland, and St Peter's College, Oxford. In 1971 he became Bishop of Waiapu, and in 1979 Bishop of Auckland. He was Primate and Archbishop of New Zealand from 1980-85, and Governor-General of New Zealand from 1985-90. He is currently in New York City as the first consultative representative of the Anglican Church at the United Nations.

*Patricia Rianne* won a New Zealand Government bursary in 1962 to study at the Royal Ballet School, London. Subsequently she danced solo with many companies, including the Royal Ballet, Marseilles Opera Ballet, Ballet Méditerranée, Ballet Rambert, Scottish Ballet and Sadlers Wells. Male dancers who have partnered her have included Rudolph Nureyev, Peter Schauffus, Jon Trimmer and Bryan Ashbridge. She has also been a choreographer and producer with the Edinburgh Festival, Hong Kong Ballet, London School of Contemporary Dance, London College of Dance, Covent Garden and the New Zealand Ballet.

*John Mansfield Thomson* was educated at Victoria University and University College, London. He was music books editor at Barrie & Jenkins, and then Faber & Faber, and edited the journals *Composer* and *Recorder and Music Magazine*. He was the founder and served for ten years as editor of *Early Music*. He became the first resident fellow of the Stout Research Centre, Wellingon, 1984-85, and was awarded the degree of DMus (Honoris causa) by Victoria University in 1991. His several books include *A Distant Music* (which won the Oxford University Press prize for biography in 1980), and *The Oxford History of New Zealand Music*.